岸本斉史

The *Naruto* comics are already at volume 10! In the blink of an eye, we've reached double digits! Although I doubt that triple digits is a milestone we'll ever achieve, it would make me exceedingly happy if all of you would continue to read and enjoy *Naruto*, without ever getting bored, for the entire run of the series!

Kishimoto, 2001

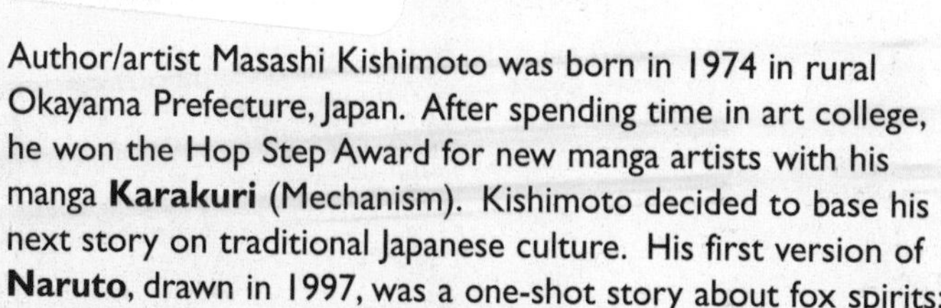

Author/artist Masashi Kishimoto was born in 1974 in rural Okayama Prefecture, Japan. After spending time in art college, he won the Hop Step Award for new manga artists with his manga **Karakuri** (Mechanism). Kishimoto decided to base his next story on traditional Japanese culture. His first version of **Naruto**, drawn in 1997, was a one-shot story about fox spirits; his final version, which debuted in **Weekly Shonen Jump** in 1999, quickly became the most popular ninja manga in Japan.

NARUTO VOL. 10
SHONEN JUMP Manga Edition

This manga contains material that was originally published in English in **SHONEN JUMP** #39–41. Artwork in the magazine may have been slightly altered from that presented here.

STORY AND ART BY MASASHI KISHIMOTO

English Adaptation/Jo Duffy, Frances E. Wall
Translation/Mari Morimoto
Touch-up Art & Lettering/Heidi Szykowny
Additional Touch-up/Josh Simpson
Design/Sean Lee
Series Editor/Joel Enos
Editor/Frances E. Wall

Printed in the U.S.A.

Published by VIZ Media, LLC
P.O. Box 77010
San Francisco, CA 94107

10 9
First printing, June 2006
Ninth printing, June 2013

viz
media
www.viz.com

RATED
T
FOR
TEEN

PARENTAL ADVISORY
NARUTO is rated T for Teen and is recommended for ages 13 and up. This volume contains realistic & fantasy violence and partial nudity.

ratings.viz.com

THE WORLD'S MOST POPULAR MANGA
SHONEN JUMP
www.shonenjump.com

SHONEN JUMP MANGA

NARUTO
殺
愛

VOL. 10

A SPLENDID NINJA

STORY AND ART BY

MASASHI KISHIMOTO

SAKURA サクラ

Smart and studious, Sakura is the brightest of Naruto's classmates, but she's constantly distracted by her crush on Sasuke. Her goal: to win Sasuke's heart!

NARUTO ナルト

When Naruto was born, a destructive fox spirit was imprisoned inside his body. Spurned by the older villagers, he's grown into an attention-seeking trouble-maker. His goal: to become the village's next *Hokage*.

SASUKE サスケ

The top student in Naruto's class, Sasuke comes from the prestigious Uchiha clan. His goal: to get revenge on a mysterious person who wronged him in the past.

Gaara 我愛羅

Bloodthirsty Gaara is one of the scariest ninja competing in the Chûnin Exams.

Rock Lee ロック・リー

Lee has been carefully observing the other students' fights while his anticipation for his own battle builds. Now it's about to begin!

FWIP

Might Guy マイト・ガイ

The flamboyant Master Guy is Lee's idol...and Kakashi's rival!

Kakashi カカシ

Although he doesn't have an especially warm personality, Kakashi is protective of his students.

Orochimaru 大蛇丸

This nefarious master of disguise placed a mysterious curse-mark on Sasuke and hopes to mold Sasuke into his successor.

Kabuto カブト

A spy for Orochimaru's village of Otogakure (The Village Hidden in the Sound), Kabuto has been living a double life in Konohagakure since childhood.

THE STORY SO FAR...

Twelve years ago, a destructive nine-tailed fox spirit attacked the ninja village of Konohagakure. The *Hokage*, or village champion, defeated the fox by sealing its soul into the body of a baby boy. Now that boy, Uzumaki Naruto, has grown up to become a ninja-in-training, learning the art of *ninjutsu* with his classmates Sakura and Sasuke.

Naruto, Sasuke and Sakura (along with six other teams of student ninja) have moved on to the third portion of the Chûnin (Journeyman Ninja) Selection Exam—a series of no-holds-barred, one-on-one bouts that begin with a set of preliminary matches. As the preliminaries continue, the battles become increasingly vicious and it's clear that lives are on the line. After the fight between Hyuga Hinata and her cousin Hyuga Neji ends with Hinata being rushed to the emergency room, tensions are at an all-time high. Then the next two combatants are announced: Rock Lee and Gaara!

NARUTO

VOL. 10
A SPLENDID NINJA

CONTENTS

Number 82: Lee's Secret!!
李
酒

SHF
...
GULP
I DON'T KNOW WHAT KIND OF TRICKS THIS BOWL-CUT KID HAS UP HIS SLEEVE...
...BUT THERE'S NO WAY HE'LL WIN AGAINST GAARA.
NO... HE'S STRONGER THAN YOU THINK...
BAM
!
FWUP

READ
THIS
WAY

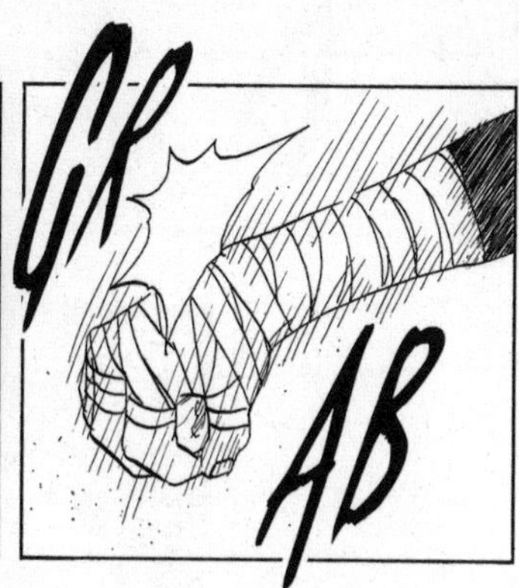
GRAB

PLEASE... DON'T RUSH THINGS.

...

ALL RIGHT, THEN. LET THE NINTH-ROUND BATTLE BEGIN!!

WATCH YOURSELF...
...LEE.

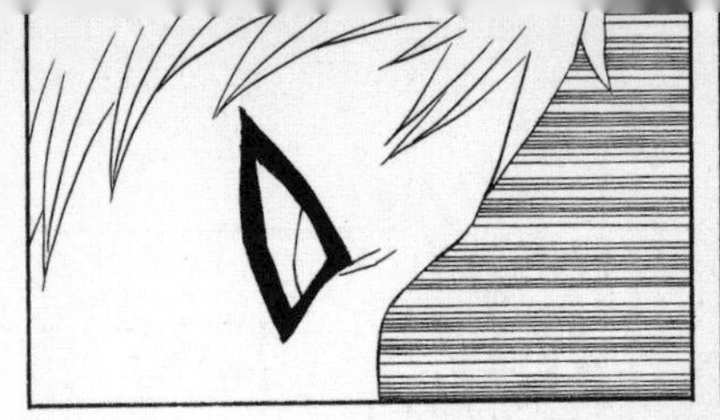

!

HEH... HE'S NO MATCH FOR GAARA.

HE MAY BE FAST...
...BUT HIS KICK WASN'T ANYTHING SPECIAL.

TAK

HOP

KONOHA HURRICANE!!!
FWSH
THOP
!!
SSSSSS
!!
...SAND ...?!
...

ZZHM!!
AGH!
TUMBLE

...SAND?!
HE'S MANIPULATING SAND?!
WHAT A CURIOUS TECHNIQUE...
THE GOURD WAS FULL OF SAND?!
DARN!
SHF

TAK
TAK
HOP
TAK

POFF
SSSH

THOP

SLITHER
SLITHER
SSHA

HUF
HUF
DARN!
WITHOUT EVEN MOVING A MUSCLE...
HUF

FAST AS HE IS, LEE IS GETTING NOWHERE!

HIS ATTACKS JUST AREN'T WORKING!
PHYSICAL ATTACKS ARE WORTHLESS AGAINST GAARA.
THE SAND FORMS A SHIELD TO PROTECT HIS BODY...
... INDEPENDENT OF GAARA'S WILL.

THAT'S WHY, TO THIS DAY, THERE'S NOT ONE PERSON...

...?
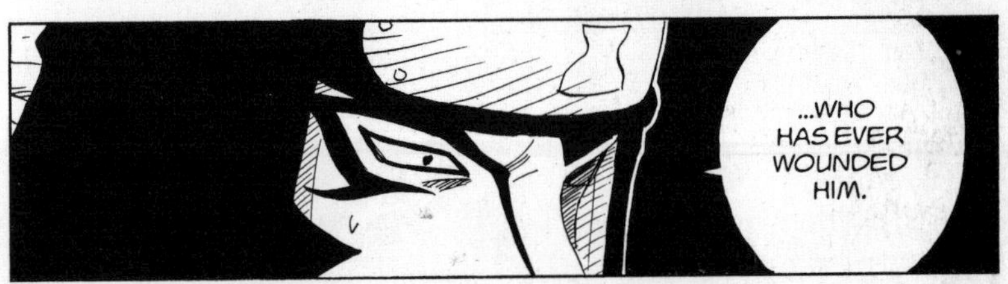
...WHO HAS EVER WOUNDED HIM.

...!
GULP
WHY IS LEE ONLY USING TAIJUTSU?!
TAIJUTSU ARE INEFFECTIVE AND PAINFUL AGAINST THAT WALL OF SAND. HE NEEDS TO USE NINJUTSU AND START ATTACKING FROM A DISTANCE!
WHOP!
UNH!
SHUP

READ THIS WAY

IT'S NOT THAT LEE WON'T USE NINJUTSU...
HUNH?

...IT'S THAT HE CAN'T.

?!
...WHAT?!

...LEE HAS PRACTICALLY NO NINJUTSU OR GENJUTSU ABILITIES...
A-ARE YOU JOKING? THEN HOW HAS HE LASTED THIS LONG?!
WHEN I FIRST MET LEE, HE HAD ABSOLUTELY NO SENSE... AND NO TALENT OR ABILITY WHATSOEVER!

THAT'S WHY THE ONLY MOVES HE'S BEEN ABLE TO DEVELOP ARE TAIJUTSU.
THERE AREN'T MANY NINJA WHO CAN USE NEITHER NINJUTSU NOR GENJUTSU...

!

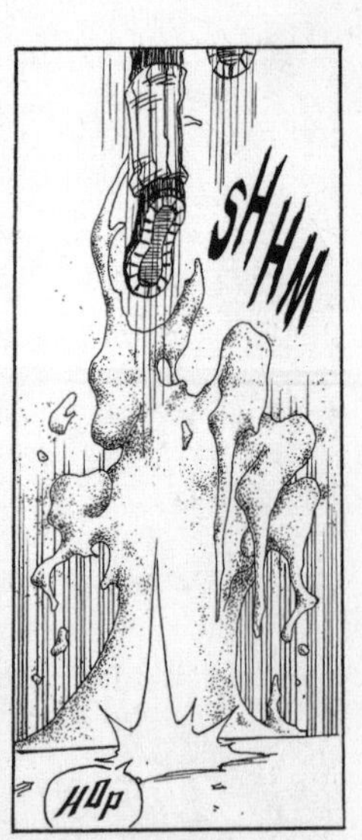
SHHM
HOP

TAK
SLITHER

HUF
HUF

READ THIS WAY

...AND THAT'S PRECISELY WHY LEE CAN WIN!

LEE! TAKE THEM OFF!!

HUH?
HM?

!

!
?

...!

B...BUT MASTER GUY! YOU SAID--
--NEVER TO DO THAT UNLESS I WAS DEFENDING THE LIVES OF PEOPLE WHO ARE PRECIOUS TO ME!!

TWIP
IT'S ALL RIGHT!!
I'LL ALLOW IT!!!

...

...
AHA... HA HA HA...

TUG

SLIP

THE CHARACTERS BELOW SAY "KONJÔ," MEANING "GUTS," "TRUE GRIT" OR "WILLPOWER."

SLIP

根性 根性 根性 根性

POK

READ
THIS
WAY

...!

GRIN

...WEIGHTS?
OH, GUY... THE MOST SICKENINGLY SWEET, SENTIMENTALLY TRADITIONAL KIND OF TRAINING!

SHF
RIGHT!!
NOW I CAN MOVE FREELY!!
SLIP
SLIP

HOW DUMB!!
I SEE!

根性
根性

HMPH... THERE'S NO WAY DROPPING A FEW WEIGHTS...
...WILL LET YOU KEEP UP WITH GAARA'S SAND...

BOOM BOOM

...
!!
!!
!!
!!

...
AREN'T YOU OVER-DOING IT, GUY?

FWIP
GO!! LEE!!

READ
THIS
WAY

YES,
SIR!!
SMOLDER
SMOLDER

FFN

!

POP

VVVVVN

!!

ALMOST!!
HE'S FAST...

WHAM
POW
BAM
SHHF

READ THIS WAY

IT'S BECAUSE HE HAD NO APTITUDE FOR EITHER NINJUTSU OR GENJUTSU...

...THAT LEE DEVOTED HIMSELF SO EXCLUSIVELY TO TAIJUTSU. ALL HIS TIME... ALL HIS ENERGY... ALL HIS FOCUS.

SO THAT EVEN IF HE LACKED ANY OTHER KIND OF ABILITIES AT ALL...
HE'D STILL BE UNBEAT-ABLE...

FWSH

...AS A TAIJUTSU SPECIALIST!!

FWSH
?!

BAM
!!
!!
!!
!
!

READ
THIS
WAY

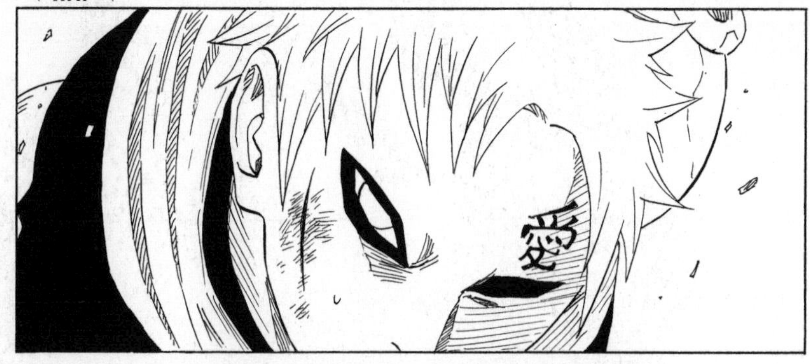
愛

IN TERMS OF SPEED, LEE CAN'T BE SURPASSED ...
I THOUGHT I GAVE YOU ALL FAIR WARNING...

...THAT THIS BOY... IS REALLY STRONG!

...

WELL... HERE WE GO!

Number 83: The Ultimate Defense... Crumbles?!

BUSHY BROWS HAS GOTTEN EVEN FASTER!!
HE REALLY IS STRONG...
...NO WAY...

IT'S UNBELIEVABLE. HE ACTUALLY MANAGED... TO WOUND GAARA!!

...!

READ
THIS
WAY

LEE!!
NOW... EXPLODE!!!

YES, SIR!!
HOP

FWWM

!

!!

OVER HERE...

FFFM

!

FWWM

KA
POW

W...WOW! HE'S SO FAST!
THE SAND BARRIER COULDN'T KEEP UP WITH HIM. IT WAS NO PROTECTION AT ALL!

I'M WEARING HIM DOWN!
HUF
SKFF
HUF
HUF

SHHF
SHHF
SLUMP

W... WOW...
GULP
HIS MOVES ARE SO FAST, MY EYES CAN'T EVEN TRACK THEM!

READ THIS WAY

YOU GOT THAT RIGHT! THAT RACCOON-EYED JERK! AFTER THE WAY HE JUST GOT HIT, HE SHOULDN'T EVEN STILL BE STANDING!!
...THIS IS BAD...

?
...THAT'S NOT THE PROBLEM...

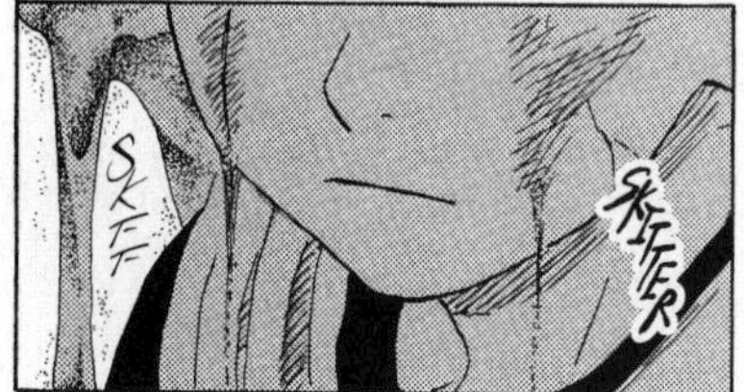
SKFF
SKITTER

...
?!

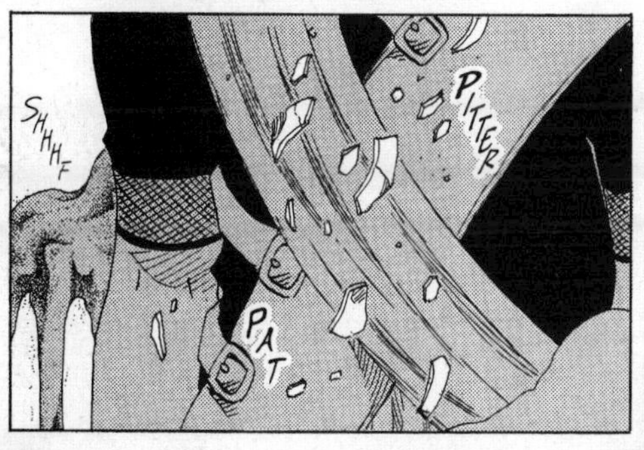
PITTER
PAT
SHHHF

!!
...WHAT...?!

愛
SNAP
POK
KRAK
SKITTER
SQUIRM
SHIVER!!

HE MUMMIFIED HIMSELF IN SAND...!
THE BLOWS BARELY TOUCHED HIM.

TREMBLE
GULP
WH... WHAT IS HE...?

WHOA! HIS WHOLE FACE JUST BROKE AND FELL OFF?!
HE WAS WEARING THE SAND LIKE A SHELL, EH...? HMM... IT'S BEEN QUITE SOME TIME SINCE I SAW THAT EXPRESSION ON HIS FACE...
HE'S USUALLY AS COMPOSED AS A STATUE, THE PICTURE OF POLITENESS AND DECORUM.
I HAD SENSED THAT, DURING THIS CHŪNIN SELECTION EXAMINATION, HE WAS BECOMING MORE AND MORE UNSTABLE... BUT...

THE OTHER GAARA...
IS NOW TOTALLY AWAKE...!
IF THIS GAARA IS ABLE TO CATCH LEE...

...
SKF

GULP

...LEE WILL BE TOYED WITH AND THEN KILLED!
...!

ZZZHZHZH

ZZH

HEY! WHAT'S THAT?! WHAT'S HE...?
IS IT SOME WAY OF PROTECTING HIMSELF FROM BUSHY BROWS?!
IT'S SAND ARMOR.

ZZH

READ THIS WAY

...ARMOR?

YES. GAARA CAN CREATE A THIN SHELL OF SAND TO COVER AND PROTECT HIS ENTIRE BODY, CONTROLLING IT BY THE FORCE OF HIS WILL.
SAND ARMOR

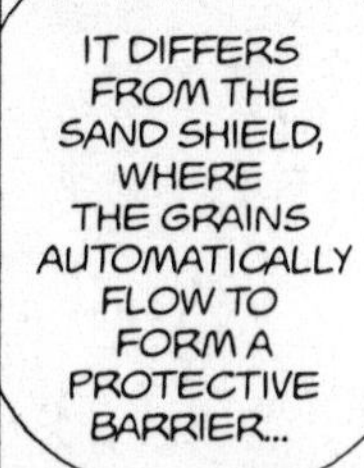
IT DIFFERS FROM THE SAND SHIELD, WHERE THE GRAINS AUTOMATICALLY FLOW TO FORM A PROTECTIVE BARRIER...
SAND SHIELD

IT'S GAARA'S...
...ULTIMATE DEFENSE!
...THEN... THERE'S NOTHING LEE CAN DO!
IT'S GOT NO WEAKNESSES...!

THAT'S NOT EXACTLY TRUE. THE SAND ARMOR IS ACTUALLY RIDDLED WITH WEAK POINTS...
IT'S HIS PROTECTION OF LAST RESORT.

IT'S NOT AUTOMATIC, THE WAY THE SHIELD IS... IT REQUIRES A MASSIVE OUTPOURING OF CHAKRA.
SWAY
ITS DEFENSIVE STRENGTH IS LESS THAN THAT OF THE SAND SHIELD... AND SINCE THE SAND ITSELF IS LYING AGAINST HIS SKIN, IT INCREASES THE WEIGHT OF HIS BODY SO HE MUST EXPEND MORE PHYSICAL STRENGTH JUST TO MOVE.
SWAY
SKITTER
SKITTER
SLITHER
愛

IF GAARA HAS BEEN DRIVEN TO USING THE ARMOR...
...THEN RIGHT NOW, HIS MIND IS PURELY ON DEFENSE. HE'S BEEN DRIVEN INTO A CORNER...!

THAT LEE IS REALLY SOME-THING!
BUT THE END OF THIS IS A FORE-GONE CONCLU-SION...

BECAUSE GAARA... IS A GENIUS!!!

IS THAT ALL...?
!

READ THIS WAY

IT'S AN AMAZING DEFENSE! HE'S ENCASED IN PROTECTION, WHICH MAKES MY SPEED IRRELEVANT...
MY ONLY SHOT IS TO JUST KEEP POUNDING AND PUNISHING THAT OUTER LAYER OF SAND!

WHAT'S HE UP TO NOW?!

LEE...

...THE LOTUS!!

NOD

HEH!

SHF

FLUTTER

FLUTTER

THE LOTUS TECHNIQUE WILL LET HIM STRIKE HIS FOE AT HIGH SPEED...

A THIN LAYER OF SAND WON'T STAND UP TO IT.

!

TAK TAK TAK TAK

AND IF IT HAPPENS THAT HE'S WEARING A THICK SHELL OF SAND, IT WILL BE ALMOST IMPOSSIBLE FOR HIM TO KICK OUTWARD...
...IN WHICH CASE...!

COME ON... HURRY UP!

KRAASK
AUGH!

AS YOU WISH!
ZOOM

AND THAT'S NOT ALL!!

TAK-TAK-TAK

THOP THOP
THOP THOP

THROB
OWW!

!!

...EVEN AN ORDINARY LOTUS MOVE EXERTS A GREAT STRAIN ON THE USER'S BODY...

THAT MANY CONSECUTIVE KICKS MAY BE TOO MUCH EVEN FOR LEE... BETTER MAKE YOUR NEXT MOVE A DECISIVE ONE, KID!!

...

GLARE

SLITHER
YANK!!

GOTCHA!!
SNAT
!!

ZZZOOON
FOR-WARD LOTUS!!

HOP
SLAM

SSS
SSSSS

...D-DO YOU THINK HE'S DEAD...?
UH... YOU'RE KIDDING, RIGHT...?!

LEE... HE...
HE WON!!

READ THIS WAY

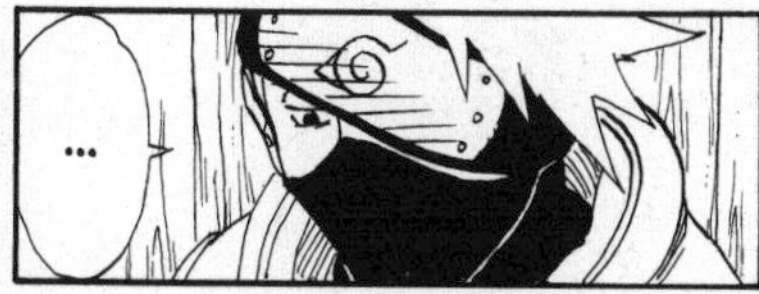
...

TAP

YES!

...

KRAK

KRAK
KRAK

PLINK
KLAT
PLINK

!
HUF
HUF
HUF
HUF

!!

SLITHER
SLITHER

!
...WHEN DID HE SLIP OUT OF THAT SHELL?!

THERE'S NO WAY HE COULD HAVE GOTTEN PAST LEE!!

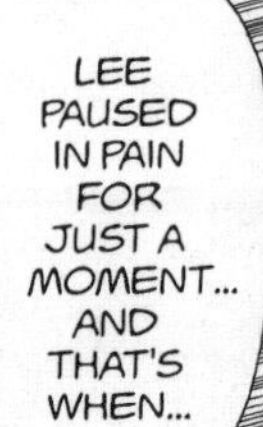
IT HAPPENED WHEN YOUR EYES WERE CLOSED IN PRAYER, GUY.
LEE PAUSED IN PAIN FOR JUST A MOMENT... AND THAT'S WHEN...

HEH HEH HEH...
SSSSHHHHHHH
SSSFFFF
!!

Number 84: The Genius of Hard Work...!!

SLITHER
SLITHER

!
!
!
IT'S FULLY AWAKENED...!

SLITHER
!!

GAARA'S INNER DEMON!

Number 84: The Genius of Hard Work!!

!!

SHUDDER
SNEAK

...!

FW
AUGH!!
SH

BAMM
UNH!

SSLIP
!
FLOP

SKF
UGH

FWAM

HUF
HUF
HUF
PLUFF

GAARA'S JUST TOYING WITH HIM...
MISTER BOWL-CUT IS AT THE END OF HIS ROPE.
POFFF

WHY DOESN'T LEE JUST DUCK?!

...

HUF
HUF
HUF
HUF

...THE LOTUS TECHNIQUE HE JUST USED... IT'S A DOUBLE-EDGED SWORD.
HUNH ?!

WHAM
AGH!
WHUD

USING THAT LEVEL OF HIGH-SPEED TAIJUTSU PUTS A HUGE STRAIN ON THE BODY...
FUNDA-MENTALLY, IT'S A FORBIDDEN MOVE.
RIGHT NOW, LEE'S NOTHING BUT A MASS OF PAIN AND WEAKNESS... ISN'T THAT RIGHT, GUY?

B-BUT... THAT MEANS...

HUF
HUF
SKF
RUMBLE
RUMBLE
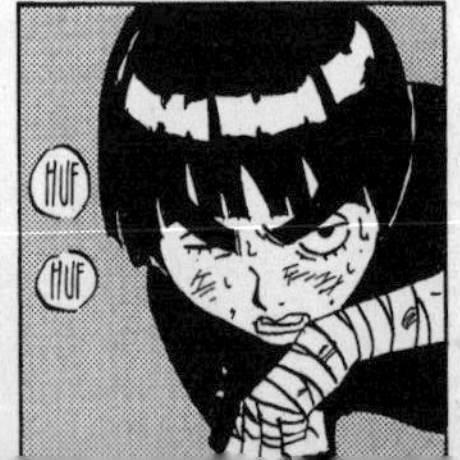
HUF
HUF

...AT THIS RATE, LEE'S GONNA...

... LEE ...

HA HA HA...
YOU IDIOT!
THERE'S NO WAY
YOU'LL EVER
BE A NINJA!
TAK

YEAH.
HOW COULD
SOMEONE WHO
CAN'T EVEN USE
NINJUTSU HOPE
TO BECOME
A NINJA?
TAK
TAK

BUT...
I WILL!!!

TAK
TAK

YOU'RE NOT
CAPABLE OF
ANYTHING BUT
TAIJUTSU... AND
YOU'RE EVEN
MEDIOCRE
AT THAT!
WHAT
WERE THEY
THINKING,
LETTING
YOU INTO
THE NINJA
ACADEMY?

HMF

HEH... WANT TO
KNOW WHAT
THE OTHER
KIDS CALL
YOU?
NO!

HA HA!!
!!
TAK TAK

STOMP STOMP
LEE! GET IN LINE!!

HEH HEH... SO THAT'S THE KID THEY'RE ALL GOSSIPING ABOUT...
...THE LITTLE **HOTHEAD** WHO COULDN'T!

SHHK

BUT LEE... YOU TOOK YOUR MEDIOCRE SKILLS IN TAIJUTSU...
...AND MADE EXERCISE AND PRACTICE YOUR OBSESSION, AND THEN...

NOW THAT YOU'VE OFFICIALLY BECOME GENIN*...
...I WANT TO HEAR ALL ABOUT YOUR GOALS!

READ THIS WAY

I DON'T WANT TO SAY.

WELL THEN...

I WANT TO BECOME A STRONG KUNOICHI, LIKE MY IDOL...
...THE LEGENDARY LADY TSUNADE!

MASTER!!
FWAP
!
EEP!

I WANT TO PROVE THAT EVEN A PERSON WHO CAN'T USE NINJUTSU OR GENJUTSU...
...CAN STILL BECOME A SPLENDID NINJA!
IT'S MY ONLY GOAL!!

HE'S GOT GOOD EYES...

HEH...
JAB
HEY! WHAT'S SO FUNNY?!

UNH...

WHAM

OH, LEE! DON'T YOU KNOW WHEN TO QUIT?
YOU DON'T STAND A CHANCE HERE... NOT AGAINST NEJI. HE'S A GENIUS...

...AND YOU'RE **NOT.**

GIVE UP, LEE.
NO MATTER HOW HARD YOU TRY, YOU CAN'T HOPE TO BEAT ME.
THAT'S JUST THE WAY IT IS.

UGH...

READ THIS WAY

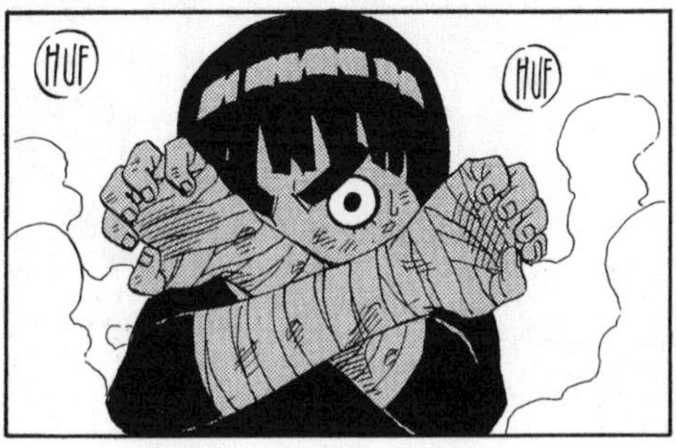

HUF
HUF

...

YEAH! YEAH! YEAH!
HUP
HUF
HUP
OKAY... IF 500 CONSECUTIVE PUSHUPS DON'T MAKE ME STRONG ENOUGH, THEN I'LL DO 1200 DOUBLE-SKIPS WITH THE JUMP ROPE...

AND IF 1200 DOUBLE-SKIPS DON'T DO IT, THEN I'LL KICK THE WOODEN PRACTICE DUMMY 2000 TIMES!
VVWN
HOP
HOP
...1116... 1117...
WHOA!
TRIP

WHUMP
...
WAH...
SOB

CHOK

OWW! UNH...

...

!
SHHF
SO, LEE... TAKING A BREAK ALREADY?

SKF
DID YOU... NEED SOMETHING, MASTER GUY?
IF IT'S ABOUT THE BLUNDER I MADE DURING THE LAST MISSION, I THOUGHT I'D ALREADY MADE IT UP TO YOU!
PAT PAT

WHAK

...

YOU KNOW... YOU REALLY ARE VERY DIFFERENT FROM NEJI...
YOU'RE NO GENIUS AT NINJUTSU OR GENJUTSU... AND YOU REALLY AREN'T A TAIJUTSU VIRTUOSO, EITHER.
NEVERTHELESS, LEE... THERE'S ONE AREA WHERE YOU COMPLETELY SURPASS NEJI.
YOU'RE A GENIUS OF ANOTHER KIND WITH GREAT HIDDEN POTENTIAL.

YOU'RE JUST SAYING THAT TO BE NICE!!
THOK

I'M NOT TRYING TO BE NICE. I'M JUST SAYING...
...THAT YOU ARE...

...

...A GENIUS OF HARD WORK.

...
...DO YOU REALLY...
...MEAN THAT?
...!

I... I'VE ONLY BEEN ABLE TO MAKE IT THIS FAR...
CLENCH
...BY HAVING FAITH THAT, IF I TRAINED TWO OR THREE TIMES AS HARD AS NEJI, I MIGHT FINALLY BEAT HIM.
I'VE ALWAYS BELIEVED THAT.
BUT... LATELY, I'VE STARTED TO FEEL THAT I HAD NO HOPE...
...OF EVER MEASURING UP TO A TRUE GENIUS LIKE NEJI.

I'VE WONDERED IF IT WAS POSSIBLE FOR HARD WORK ALONE TO BE REWARDED...
...SO I'VE KEPT CHALLENG-ING NEJI... BUT THE RESULTS HAVE ALWAYS BEEN THE SAME...
I'M NO MATCH FOR HIM!
AND EVEN NOW, ON MISSIONS, MY LEGS STILL TREMBLE IN FEAR...
...FEAR THAT NO MATTER HOW HARD I WORK, I'LL NEVER GET STRONGER.
SMAK
IT SCARES ME SO MUCH I CAN'T STAND IT.
PLIT PLIT
...
...I DON'T KNOW WHAT TO DO...

ALL YOUR HARD WORK WILL PROVE WORTHLESS...

...UNLESS YOU BELIEVE IN YOURSELF!

HUF
PEEK
HUF

...!

THANK YOU... MASTER GUY...
...
TINK...

Number 85: Now, of All Times...!!

...THE LOTUS OF KONOHA WILL BLOOM TWICE...
...

THE FIGHTING LOTUS OF KONOHA WILL GROW AND FLOWER AGAIN!
BEFORE WE MEET AGAIN, I WILL HAVE BECOME A STRONGER MAN.
I SWEAR IT!

SHH

...FOR YOU, IT ENDS HERE.

WELL, ONE WAY OR ANOTHER...
...THE NEXT MOVE WILL BE THE LAST.

READ THIS WAY

THE LOTUS OF KONOHA WILL BLOOM TWICE?

GUY... DON'T TELL ME YOU...!

ON THE CONTRARY. I DID.

...!

THEN... THAT KID, WHO'S JUST A GENIN...
...IS ABLE TO OPEN THE EIGHT INNER GATES...?

YES...
...THAT'S RIGHT.

IT'S AWFUL...
?

HE HAS THE TALENT...
NO MATTER HOW MUCH TALENT HE HAS, YOU TAUGHT HIM SOMETHING HORRIBLY DANGEROUS!

THE REVERSE LOTUS TOPS THE LIST...
...OF MOVES THAT YOU SHOULDN'T TEACH!!

!!
...REVERSE LOTUS...?

IT'S NONE OF MY BUSINESS WHAT THAT CHILD MEANS TO YOU...
...AND I'LL SPARE US BOTH THE LECTURE ABOUT NOT BEING GOVERNED BY YOUR FEELINGS... BUT YOU CROSSED A LINE ON THIS!
...YOU DISAPPOINT ME, GUY!
...
YOU...
...DON'T KNOW THE FIRST THING ABOUT THAT KID...

I WANT TO PROVE THAT EVEN A PERSON WHO CAN'T USE NINJUTSU OR GENJUTSU...
...CAN STILL BECOME A SPLENDID NINJA! IT'S MY ONLY GOAL!!

THAT BOY HAS SOMETHING HE VALUES SO DEEPLY THAT HE'S WILLING TO DIE FOR THE SAKE OF IT.
THAT'S WHY I... WANTED TO HELP HIM BECOME SOMEONE WHO'D BE ABLE TO STAND UP FOR HIS IDEALS.
I HAD TO.

...LEE... I'D LIKE TO SHOW YOU SOMETHING NEW...
...A MOVE THAT CAN BECOME YOUR ACE IN THE HOLE.
HUNH?
YOU BET I DID!!
OH BOY...
...THIS IS GREAT!!!
LEE, DID YOU HEAR ME?
LEE!
SNAP OUT OF IT AND PAY ATTENTION!!

YIPE!
Y-YES, SIR!

I'VE GOT TO START BY WARNING YOU THAT THIS MOVE IS EVEN MORE FORBIDDEN THAN THE LOTUS...
...AND IT WILL BECOME A VERY SPECIAL MOVE IN YOUR ARSENAL.

...!
...SPECIAL...

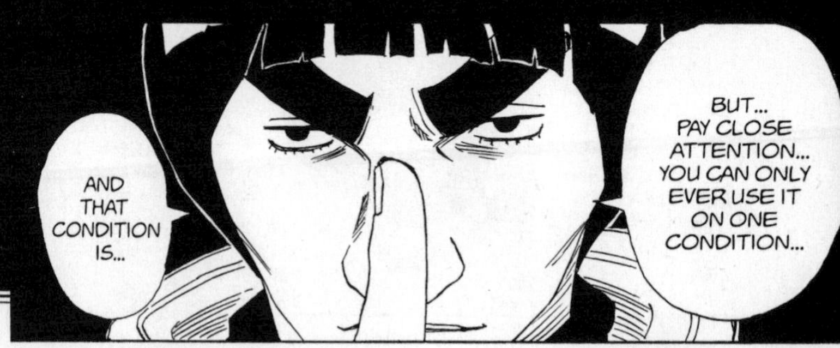
BUT... PAY CLOSE ATTENTION... YOU CAN ONLY EVER USE IT ON ONE CONDITION...
AND THAT CONDITION IS...

SHHF

SO HE WAS ABLE TO BOUNCE BACK FROM EXHAUSTION WITH SUCH ABNORMAL SPEED BECAUSE HE'D FORCED OPEN THE KYUMON -- THE GATE OF REST.
SO TELL ME, GUY... WHICH OF THE EIGHT INNER GATES HAS HE GOTTEN UP TO SO FAR?
THE FIFTH GATE.

!!!

?!

THAT FEAT SHOULD BE IMPOSSIBLE TO ACHIEVE THROUGH HARD WORK ALONE...
SO... THE BOY'S A GENIUS AFTER ALL.

WH... WHAT ARE YOU BOTH TALKING ABOUT?!
YOU KEEP MENTIONING THESE... INNER GATES?

THE GATES ACT AS LIMITERS THAT MUST BE RELEASED IN PREPARATION FOR PERFORMING THE REVERSE LOTUS.
LIMITERS... RELEASED?

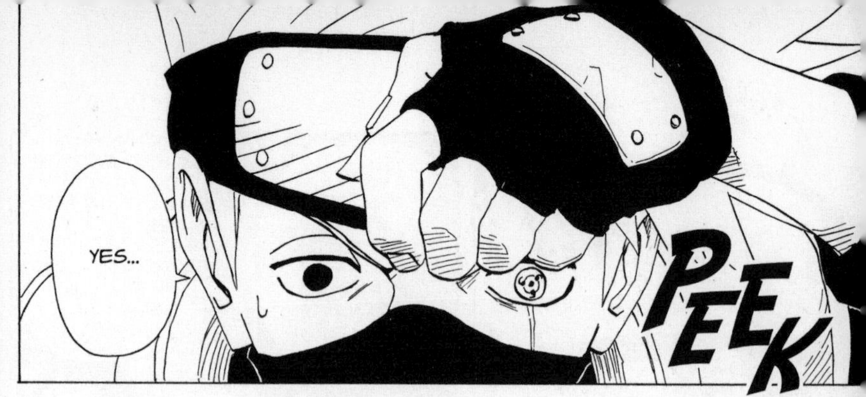
PEEK
YES...

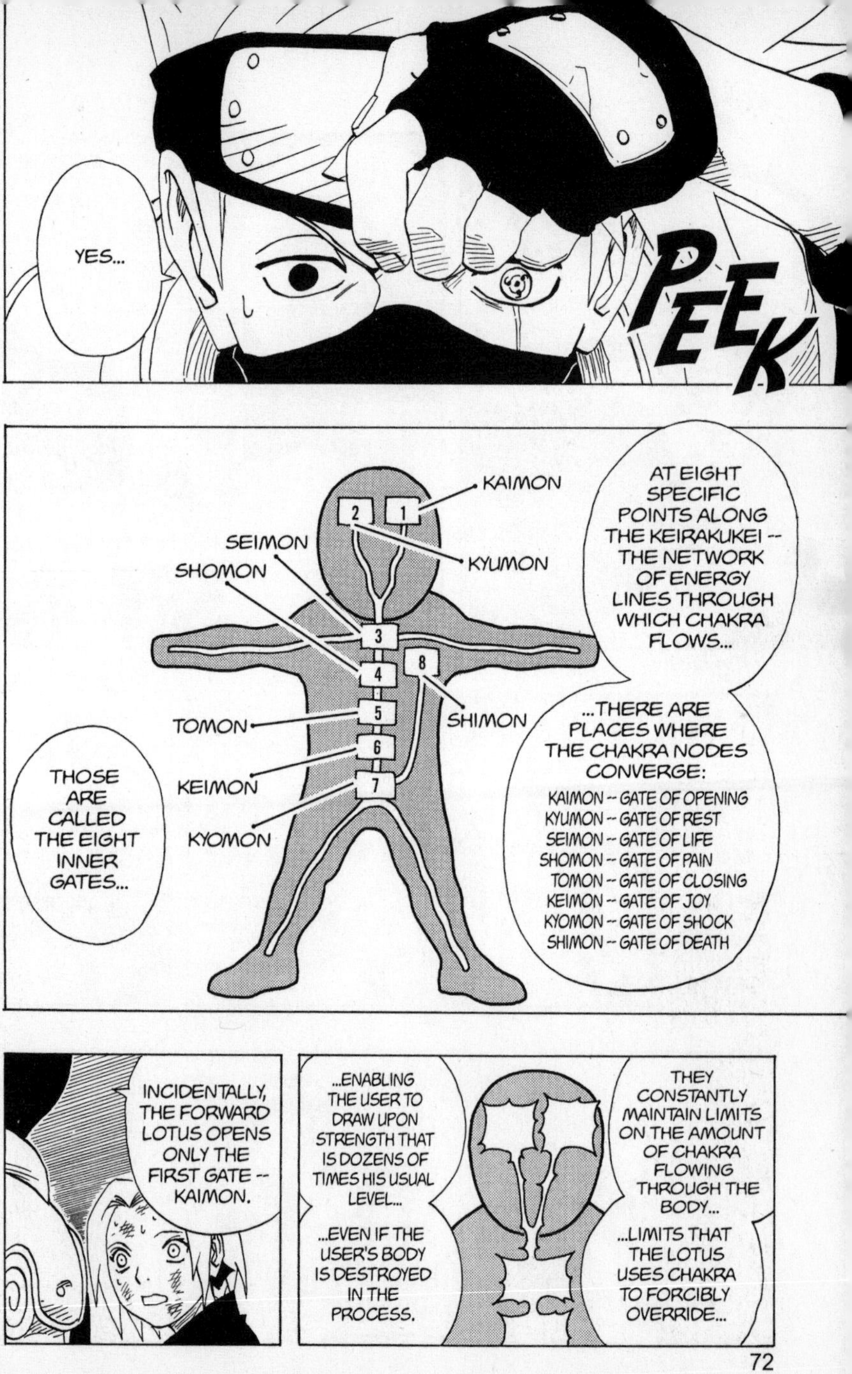

AT EIGHT SPECIFIC POINTS ALONG THE KEIRAKUKEI -- THE NETWORK OF ENERGY LINES THROUGH WHICH CHAKRA FLOWS...

...THERE ARE PLACES WHERE THE CHAKRA NODES CONVERGE:
KAIMON -- GATE OF OPENING
KYUMON -- GATE OF REST
SEIMON -- GATE OF LIFE
SHOMON -- GATE OF PAIN
TOMON -- GATE OF CLOSING
KEIMON -- GATE OF JOY
KYOMON -- GATE OF SHOCK
SHIMON -- GATE OF DEATH

1 KAIMON
2 KYUMON
3 SEIMON
4 SHOMON
5 TOMON
6 KEIMON
7 KYOMON
8 SHIMON

THOSE ARE CALLED THE EIGHT INNER GATES...

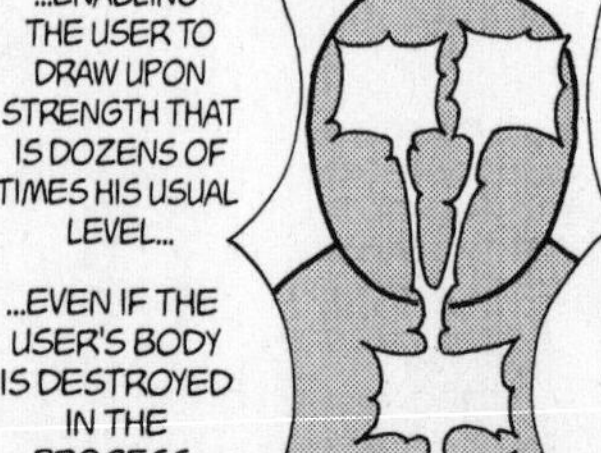
THEY CONSTANTLY MAINTAIN LIMITS ON THE AMOUNT OF CHAKRA FLOWING THROUGH THE BODY...
...LIMITS THAT THE LOTUS USES CHAKRA TO FORCIBLY OVERRIDE...
...ENABLING THE USER TO DRAW UPON STRENGTH THAT IS DOZENS OF TIMES HIS USUAL LEVEL...
...EVEN IF THE USER'S BODY IS DESTROYED IN THE PROCESS.

INCIDENTALLY, THE FORWARD LOTUS OPENS ONLY THE FIRST GATE -- KAIMON.

READ THIS WAY

...!
AND... THE REVERSE LOTUS?

OPENING THE KAIMON FREES THE USER FROM HIS OWN MENTAL INHIBITIONS. THE OPENING OF THE KYUMON BOOSTS HIS STRENGTH...
...AND WITH THE OPENING OF THE THIRD GATE --THE SEIMON -- ONE CAN BEGIN THE REVERSE LOTUS...

BUT... THE FORWARD LOTUS ALONE GOT HIM SO BEATEN UP...
...IF HE TRIES TO PERFORM ANY MORE MOVES...

THAT'S RIGHT... THIS TECHNIQUE TRULY IS A DOUBLE-EDGED SWORD.
THE STATE WHERE ALL THE GATES HAVE BEEN OPENED IS CALLED THE "EIGHT INNER GATES FORMATION"...
...AND ANYONE WHO ACHIEVES THAT STATE WILL, HOWEVER BRIEFLY, BE GRANTED STRENGTH THAT SURPASSES EVEN THE HOKAGE'S. BUT IN EXCHANGE...

!!
...THAT PERSON WILL INEVITABLY DIE!

FLASH

!
愛

AND EVEN...
...SASUKE...
...NEJI...

MASTER GUY... PLEASE... NOTICE ME...
...NOW, OF ALL TIMES...

I WILL NOT BE...
...THE ONLY ONE WHO FAILS!!

...NOW, WHEN I FINALLY ATTAIN...
...MY SHINOBI PATH!!!
THE THIRD GATE, SEIMON... RELEASE!!

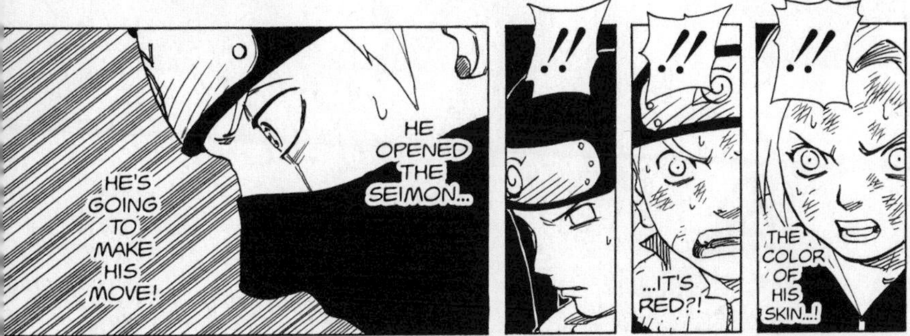
!!
THE COLOR OF HIS SKIN...!
!!
...IT'S RED?!
!!
HE OPENED THE SEIMON...
HE'S GOING TO MAKE HIS MOVE!

AND, WHILE I'M AT IT... THE FOURTH GATE, SHOMON... RELEASE!!!

HYAAAH!!!

DRIP

HE'S QUITE SOMETHING...

...

TAK

!!

RUMBLE

SLAM

SMASH!!

HE'S FAST!!
CRAK
CRAK

OW!
YAAH!

WHERE DID HE GO?!
GAARA?!

LOOK UP!
BUT WHAT ABOUT LEE?! I DON'T SEE HIM ANYWHERE!

SWOOOP

CRUMBLE

NOW IT LOOKS LIKE THE SAND...
...JUST CAN'T KEEP UP!
WHF
!
SNAP
SNAP
WHUF
AGH!
BANG

POW POW POW POW

WHAK

WHAT?! MY SAND ARMOR IS...

...PEELING OFF?!

TKSH

THE SAND ARMOR AGAIN, EH?

AT THIS RATE...

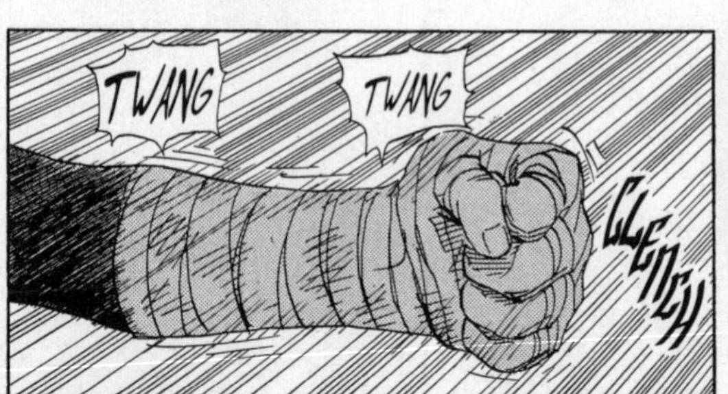
TWANG
TWANG
CLENCH

READ THIS WAY

HIS MUSCLES HAVE TORN...
IF THIS GOES ANY FARTHER...

BUT... IT'S ONLY LEE! HOW DID HE GET SO...?

FLINCH

!!

ROAR

THIS IS THE END!!

THE FIFTH GATE, TOMON... RELEASE!!!

THE WORLD OF KISHIMOTO MASASHI
MY PERSONAL HISTORY, PART 12

IN MIDDLE SCHOOL, I WAS SO FOCUSED ON BASEBALL THAT I ALMOST STOPPED DRAWING COMPLETELY.
THERE WERE GAMES EVERY SATURDAY AND SUNDAY, AND PRACTICE EVERY WEEKDAY MORNING. EVEN MY AFTER-SCHOOL TIME WAS FILLED WITH HOURS OF CRAM SCHOOL, SO I WAS ALWAYS INCREDIBLY BUSY. IT WAS LIKE ANOTHER WORLD COMPARED TO ELEMENTARY SCHOOL, AND ALL OF THE TIME I HAD ONCE SPENT DRAWING WAS GONE.
ONE DAY, JUST WHEN I WAS STARTING TO THINK, "MAYBE I'VE OUTGROWN THE URGE TO BE DRAWING ALL THE TIME," I HAD A SUDDEN AND INCREDIBLE REVELATION. IT WAS SO AMAZING THAT I STILL LOOK BACK ON THAT MOMENT AS A HUGE TURNING POINT. THE AMAZING MOMENT OCCURRED WHEN I SAW A MOVIE POSTER.
I WAS ON MY WAY HOME ONE DAY WHEN I HAPPENED TO GLANCE AT A POSTER FOR OTOMO KATSUHIRO'S *AKIRA*.
IN AN INSTANT, THE SIGHT OF IT HAD AN IMPACT ON ME SO POWERFUL THAT EVEN NOW IT'S HARD TO DESCRIBE. I STOOD STARING AT IT FOR OVER AN HOUR. THE POSTER FEATURED AN OVERHEAD SHOT OF THE MAIN CHARACTER, KANEDA, WALKING TOWARDS A MOTORCYCLE. THE COMPOSITION OF IT WAS INCREDIBLY COMPLEX. "HOW DID THIS GUY DRAW ANYTHING SO COMPLICATED THAT WELL?" "I'VE NEVER KNOWN ANYONE WHO COULD HAVE MADE THAT COMPOSITION WORK..."
DESPITE THE TRICKY ANGLES OF THE PERSPECTIVE, THE BIKE AND KANEDA WERE BOTH DRAWN PERFECTLY, WITH ALL THE SPATIAL RELATIONSHIPS CORRECT. THE SENSE THAT KANEDA WAS ACTUALLY STANDING SOLIDLY ON THE GROUND WAS CONVEYED IN A WAY THAT SEEMED TOTALLY REAL AND COOL. THE BIKE HAD AN AMAZING DESIGN, AND THERE WERE CRACKS IN THE GROUND AND PEBBLES SCATTERED ABOUT, SEEMINGLY AT RANDOM. THAT POSTER SEEMED LIKE THE COOLEST, MOST ORIGINAL THING I HAD EVER SEEN AND IT REKINDLED THE FLAME OF MY ARTISTIC PASSION.
EVER SINCE THAT DAY, I'VE KEPT DRAWING WITH THE HOPE THAT SOMEDAY I CAN APPROACH THE STANDARD SET BY THAT PICTURE.

!
Number 86: A Splendid Ninja...!!

HEY, NEJI! THIS IS A MOVE I WAS KEEPING IN RESERVE TO USE AGAINST YOU, BUT...
SHF
...I'LL GIVE YOU A SNEAK PREVIEW!

MY DEFENSES ARE FAILING...
IS HE EVEN HUMAN...?!

THUD

KRAK
SWF

!!

CLENCH

SSSSSS
SSS

THE SAND SHIELD CAN'T KEEP UP...
MUCH OF THE SAND ARMOR HAS BEEN TORN AWAY!...
THIS IS NOT GOOD...!!
THE REVERSE LOTUS... A SERIES OF TAIJUTSU PERFORMED WITH SUCH SPEED THAT THE ATTACKER IS UNTOUCHABLE!
THESE RAPID MOVES ARE LEE'S KEY TO WINNING THE MATCH...
THERE'S NO WAY THE SAND CAN CATCH UP...!
...
THIS IS THE FINALE!
GRIP
YANK
HYAH!!
FWOOM
!!

Number 86:
REVERSE LOTUS!!!
A Splendid Ninja...!!

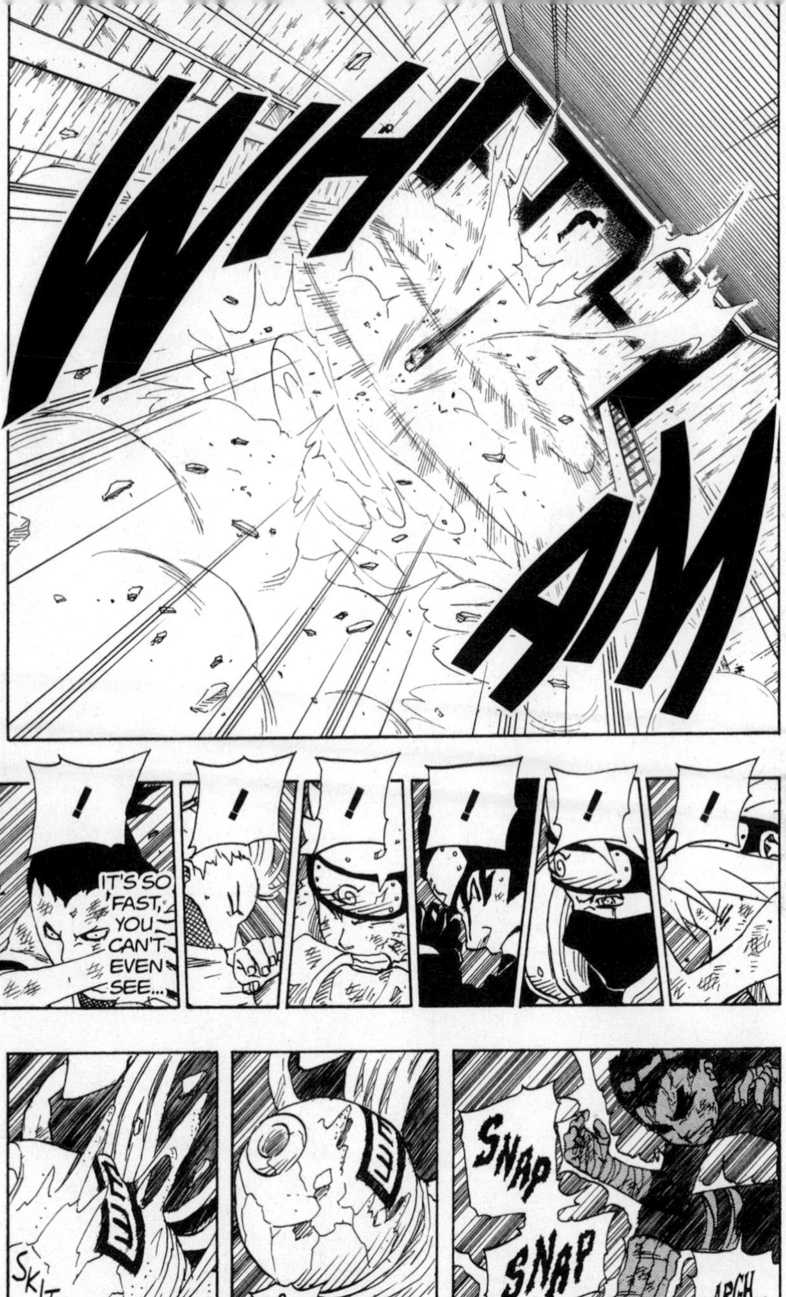

WHAM

!
!
!
!
!
!
IT'S SO FAST, YOU CAN'T EVEN SEE...

SNAP
SNAP
ARGH...

KRAK

SKITTER

THE GOURD IS TURNING TO SAND...!
!

DON'T TELL ME...
!

KABOOM

CLATTER
CLATTER

CLATTER

ARGH!!
THUD
SKIDDD

TWTCH
HUF
HUF
SHF

!!
THE GOURD... WAS MADE OF SAND...
...HE USED IT TO PROTECT HIMSELF!

SHM
MM
!!

!!
BLINK

TAK
SWM

!
THAT MOVE... IT'S...!!

CLENCH

SABAKUKYÛ! THE COFFIN OF CRUSHING SAND!!

!!

!!

!

!

!

BLINK

AAGH!!

SNAP

SNAP

READ
THIS
WAY

SSSHMN

...!

HUF

HUF

HUF

...!

FWASH

!!

...!

TWIK

CHR
OB
UNH...

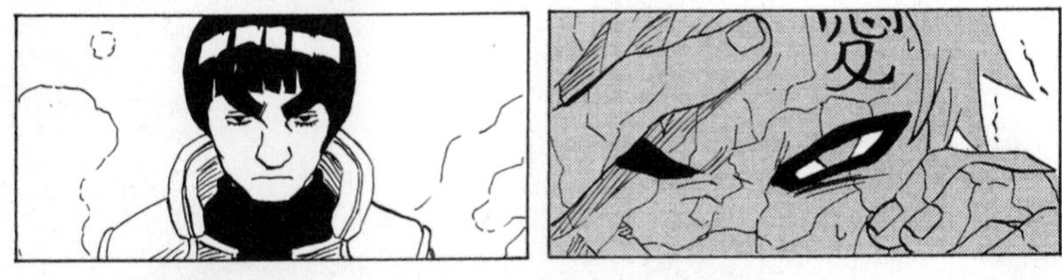

WHY ARE YOU...
...HELPING HIM?

SIZZLE
SZZ
HEH HEH... I'M ALL RIGHT...
...'CAUSE I'M SO STRONG!

WHOP
WHAK
MASTER GUY, I'LL EXCEL IN THE CHŪNIN EXAM... YOU CAN SIT BACK AND ENJOY THE SHOW!

I WANT TO PROVE THAT EVEN A PERSON WHO CAN'T USE NINJUTSU OR GENJUTSU...
...CAN STILL BECOME A SPLENDID NINJA! IT'S MY ONLY GOAL!!

HE'S...

READ THIS WAY

HE'S MY LOVABLE, PRECIOUS PROTÉGÉ!

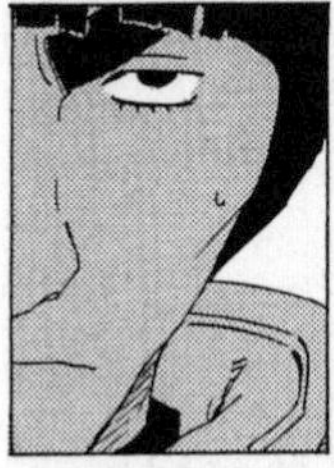

...THOSE WORDS ARE BEYOND THE SCOPE OF GAARA'S UNDER-STANDING...

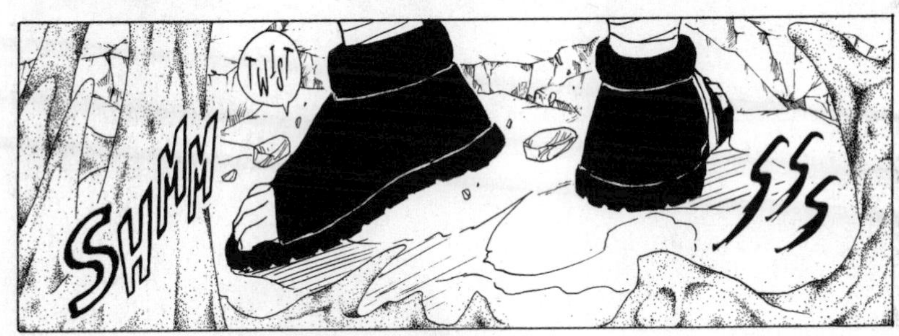
TWIST
SSS
SHMM

SSS
SHM
FORGET IT...

THE VICTOR IS GAARA!
SHM

HUH?!

...!

!

I CAN'T BELIEVE IT...

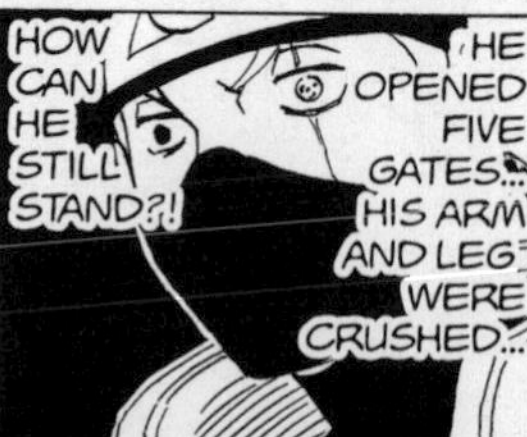
HE OPENED FIVE GATES... HIS ARM AND LEG WERE CRUSHED...
HOW CAN HE STILL STAND?!

KREAK
TREMBLE
KRK
POP
KREAK

READ THIS WAY

LEE, IT'S ALL RIGHT... IT'S OVER.
YOU'RE IN NO SHAPE TO BE STANDING...
WOBBLE
PAT

!

...LEE... YOU...
...

DRIP

...YOU INCREDIBLE KID...

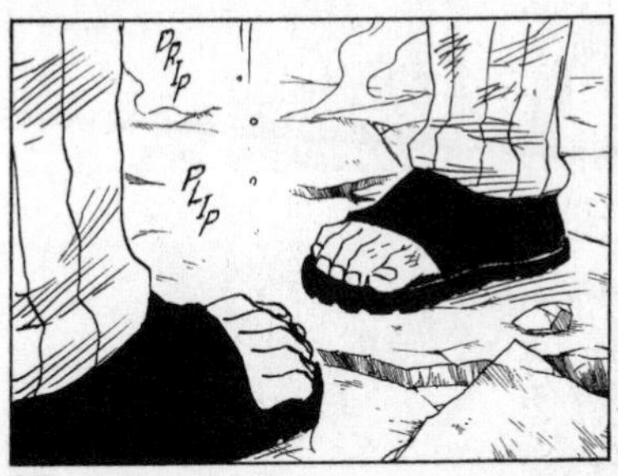
DRIP
PLIP

EVEN THOUGH YOU'VE BEEN KNOCKED SENSELESS, YOU'RE STILL...
...TRYING TO STAY TRUE TO YOUR SHINOBI PATH...

LEE...
YOU ARE AL-READY ...

READ THIS WAY

!
MASTER GUY IS SITTING BACK AND ENJOYING THE SHOW...
RATTLE
...JUST KNOWING THAT IS ENOUGH TO REVIVE ME...!
SHHF

...AND TO MAKE ME...
...STRONGER THAN EVER!
FWUP

LEE'S BEING PUSHED AROUND SO BRUTALLY... WHY IS HE SMILING?
HE'S ABOUT TO START PUSHING BACK!

HUH?

THE LOTUS OF KONOHA...
...WILL BLOOM TWICE!!

MASASHI
KO-RA
NA RU TO
KISHIMOTO

READ
THIS
WAY

SQUEEZE...

...A SPLENDID NINJA...!

...

• THIS CHARACTER IS FROM AN UNPUBLISHED WORK I DID PRIOR TO NARUTO.

Number 87: The Preliminaries... Completed!!

愛

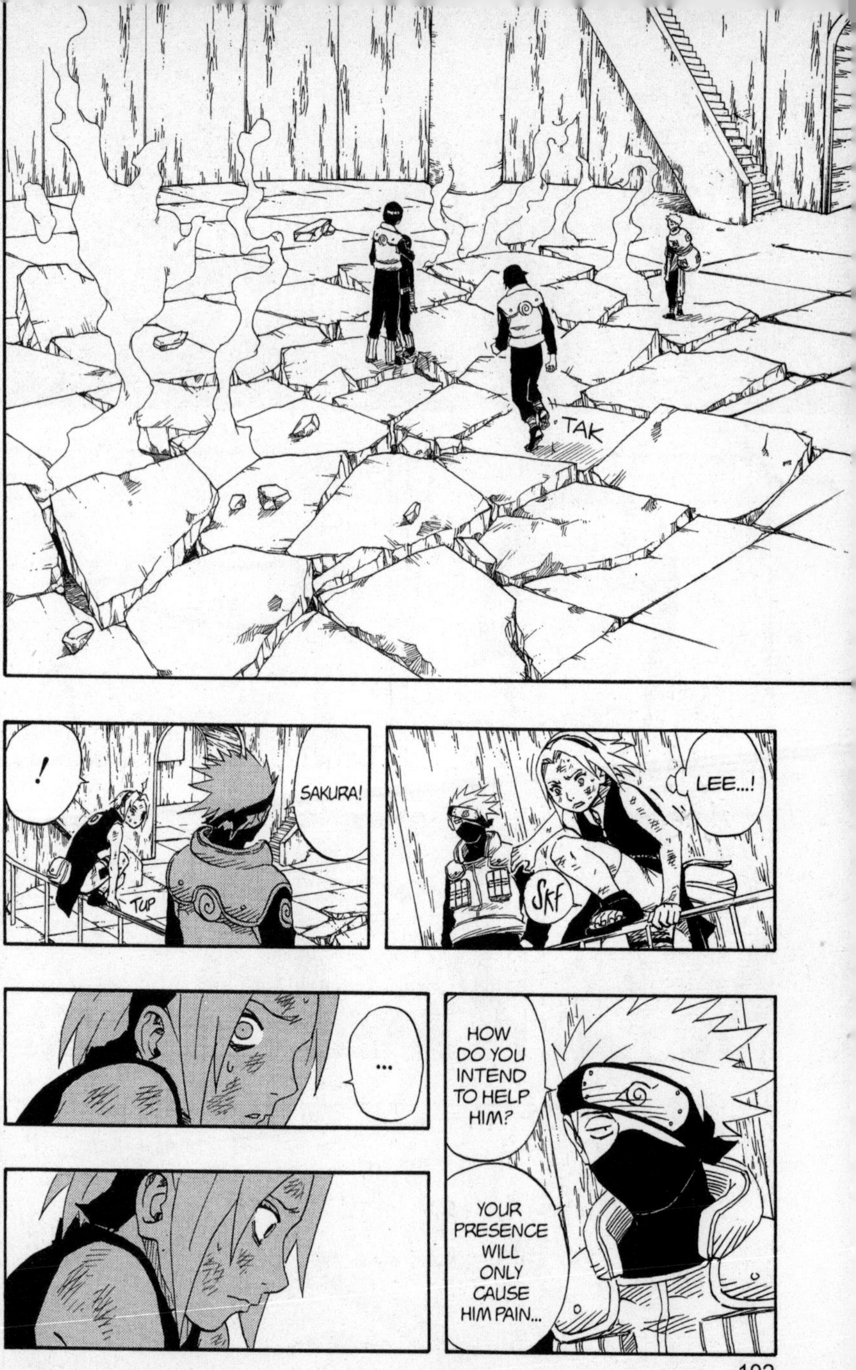

TAK

LEE...!
SKF

SAKURA!
!
TUP

HOW DO YOU INTEND TO HELP HIM?
YOUR PRESENCE WILL ONLY CAUSE HIM PAIN...

...

WHSH
SKF
...LEE, NO! GIVE UP BEFORE HE KILLS YOU!!
HOP
BAM

!
!
!
!
!
HE GOT HIS SPEED BACK!!

YOU REMIND ME OF ME... WAY BACK WHEN I WAS A COMPLETE FAILURE.

NOWADAYS, IN MATCHES AGAINST THAT ELITE GENIUS, KAKASHI, WE'RE NEARLY EVEN!!

!

"I WANT TO PROVE THAT EVEN A PERSON WHO CAN'T USE NINJUTSU OR GENJUTSU CAN STILL BECOME A SPLENDID NINJA!"

THAT'S YOUR SHINOBI PATH, ISN'T IT?

IT'S A GREAT GOAL...

...ONE THAT'S REALLY WORTH FIGHTING FOR.

...!

IT'S THE PATH YOU CHOSE, SO HAVE FAITH AND FOLLOW IT!

BECOME SUCH A STRONG FIGHTER THAT I CAN JUST SIT BACK AND ENJOY THE SHOW!

YOU GOT THAT, LEE?!
YES, SIR!!

READ THIS WAY

SHF

HMPH! HE NEVER HAD A CHANCE AGAINST GAARA...

!
HOP

TAK

HOW COULD BUSHY BROWS LOSE TO SUCH A JERK?!

NARUTO...

EMERGENCY UNIT, PLEASE HURRY!!
TAK TAK

E...
EXCUSE
US!

...

!

ARE YOU
THE JÔNIN
RESPONSIBLE
FOR HIM?
IF I MAY HAVE
A WORD...
!

READ THIS WAY

...THOUGH HE'S BREATHING ON HIS OWN, HE HAS COMPOUND COMPRESSIVE FRACTURES AND TORN MUSCLES THROUGHOUT HIS BODY.
IF THAT WERE THE FULL EXTENT OF HIS INJURIES, WE COULD STILL EXPECT A FULL RECOVERY, BUT...
...THE DAMAGE TO HIS ATTACKED LEFT ARM AND LEG IS ESPECIALLY SEVERE.

I DON'T WANT TO SAY THIS, BUT...

...

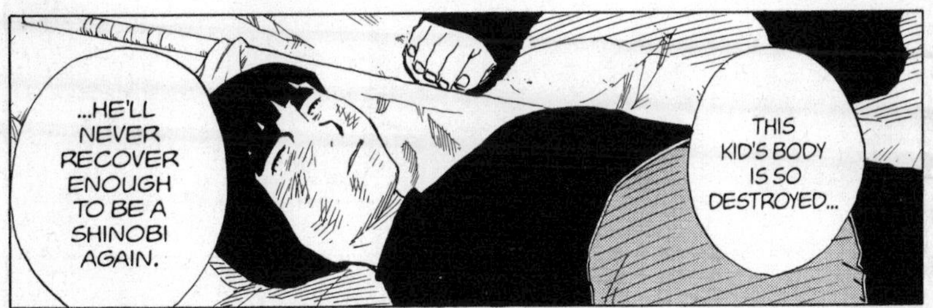
THIS KID'S BODY IS SO DESTROYED...
...HE'LL NEVER RECOVER ENOUGH TO BE A SHINOBI AGAIN.

!!

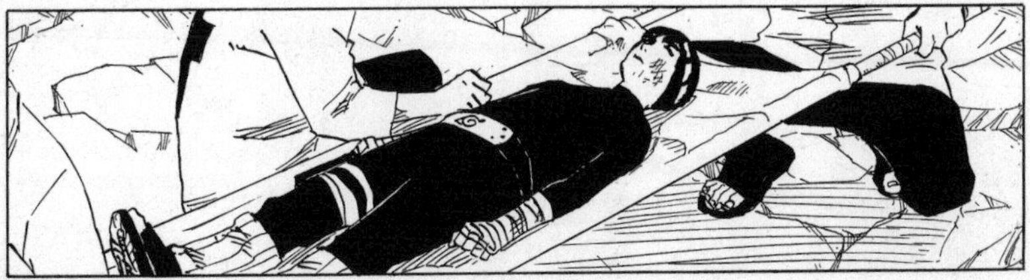

N... NO WAY...
YOU MUST BE KIDDING...

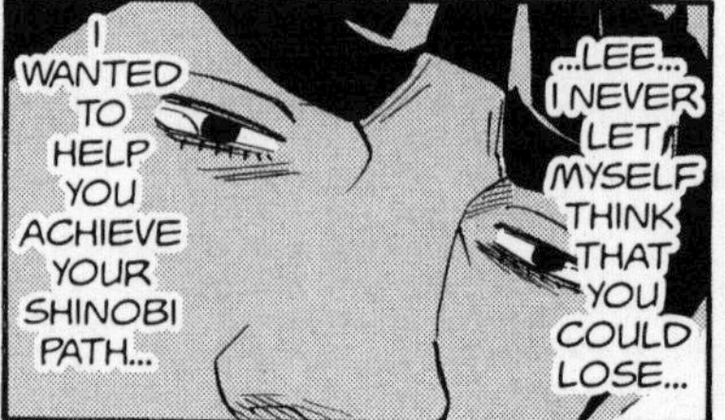
...LEE... I NEVER LET MYSELF THINK THAT YOU COULD LOSE...
I WANTED TO HELP YOU ACHIEVE YOUR SHINOBI PATH...

...PLEASE FORGIVE ME, LEE... FOR NOT STOPPING YOU...
...BEFORE IT WAS TOO LATE.

WELL...
WHAT IS BUSHY BROWS SUPPOSED TO DO?!
HE KEPT SAYING HE WAS DESPERATE TO FIGHT SASUKE AND THAT NEJI GUY...
CAN'T YOU DO ANY-THING TO HELP HIM?!

HEY...!
CLAMP
MPH!

READ THIS WAY

...BUT MAYBE...
...THAT WAS HIS UN-DOING.
...!

IT WAS HIS OWN CHOICE TO USE A FORBIDDEN, SELF-SACRIFICING ART...
...IN A LAST-DITCH EFFORT TO WIN.

HE SACRIFICED HIMSELF TO HONOR...
...THE UN-SPOKEN OATH...

...THE OATH THAT EXISTS BETWEEN HIM AND SASUKE, NEJI... AND EVEN YOU, NARUTO...
...
HE RISKED HIS LIFE...
...SO THAT HE MIGHT HAVE THE CHANCE TO FIGHT ALL OF YOU.

...DON'T FORGET THAT.

...

LEE...
EVEN AT THE BITTER END, YOU DIDN'T REALIZE...

...THE HEAVENS WOULD NEVER ALLOW YOU TO ADVANCE FURTHER...
...IF YOUR TRIUMPH WERE A PYRRHIC VICTORY.

READ THIS WAY

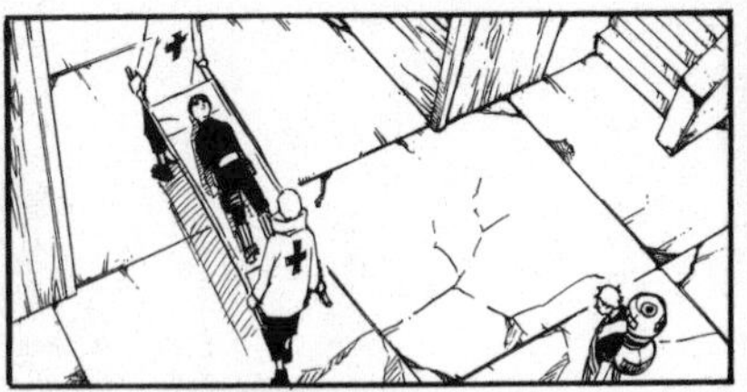

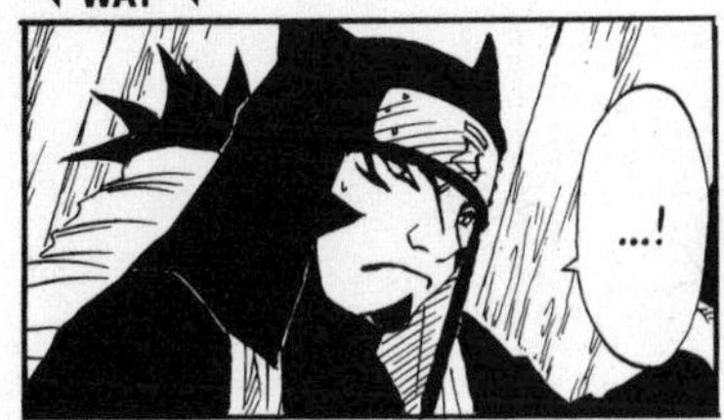
...!

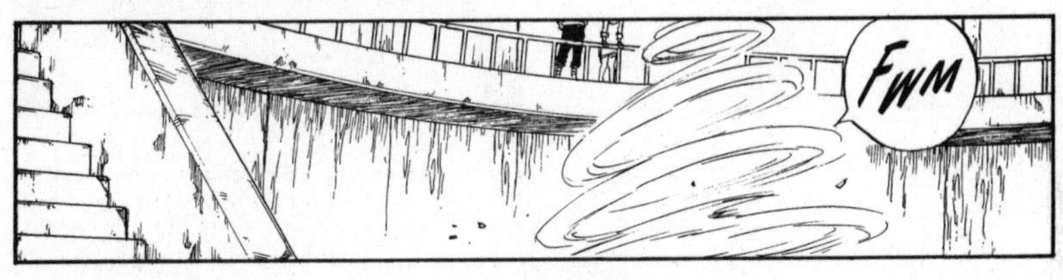
FWM

!

SWIRL

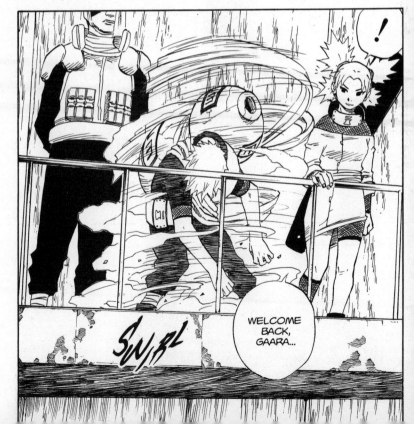

WELCOME BACK, GAARA...

GUY...
...

...I WAS PRETTY COCKY EARLIER, BUT... TO BE HONEST...
...IF I'D BEEN IN YOUR POSITION...
...I PROBABLY WOULDN'T HAVE BEEN ABLE TO STOP LEE EITHER.

!

GUY...
WE'RE IN THE WAY.
LET'S GO BACK UPSTAIRS...

...
YEAH...

READ THIS WAY

WELL... IT'S THE FINALE... THE 10TH ROUND BATTLE.
BOTH CON-TESTANTS, PLEASE STEP FORWARD!

LOOKS LIKE I'M LAST...

IN ANY CASE, I'VE GOT TO MAKE IT TO THE FINALS AND FIGHT SASUKE...
...OTHERWISE I'LL FAIL TO MEET YOUR EXPECTATIONS, LORD OROCHIMARU.

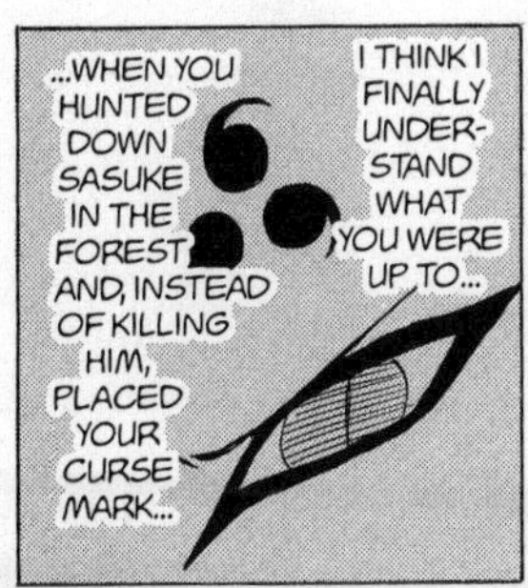
I THINK I FINALLY UNDER-STAND WHAT YOU WERE UP TO...
...WHEN YOU HUNTED DOWN SASUKE IN THE FOREST AND, INSTEAD OF KILLING HIM, PLACED YOUR CURSE MARK...

THE THREE OF US SERVED AS YOUR GUINEA PIGS. YOU SENT US AFTER SASUKE WITH ASSASSINATION ORDERS... BUT REALLY YOU JUST INTENDED FOR US TO FIGHT HIM...
...TO TEST HIS ABILITIES AND EXPERIENCE THEM FIRSTHAND. WHAT YOU WANT IS NOT SASUKE'S LIFE, BUT SASUKE HIMSELF...

YOU'VE BEEN TOYING WITH ME, TOO...
HOP

FWSH

UH... WELL... LET THE 10TH ROUND BATTLE BEGIN!

GO GET HIM!
YOU CAN DO IT, FATSO!!

UGH...! SHUT YOUR MOUTH AND KEEP YOUR EYES OPEN!
I'M GONNA END THIS MATCH FAST SO I CAN COME BEAT YOU UP!

...WELL THEN...
...I'LL DISPENSE WITH THE GAMES AND QUICKLY FINISH IT FOR YOU, FATSO!

READ THIS WAY

YOU MUMMIFIED, RAIN-PONCHO-WEARING CREEP...!
I FOUGHT YOU BEFORE, SO I ALREADY KNOW YOUR WEAKNESSES!
YOU RELEASE SOUND WAVES FROM THOSE HOLES IN YOUR ARM, SO...
NINJA TECHNIQUE: BAIKA NO JUTSU! THE ART OF EXPANSION!!

POOF

SHWMP
AS LONG AS I PROTECT MY EARS...

FWRLLL

I'M PLEASINGLY PLUMP!!

NIKUDAN SENSHA! THE HUMAN JUGGERNAUT!!

ALL RIGHT! CRUSH HIM, CHOJI!!

...

CHOJI'S HEAD IS BURIED WITHIN HIS BODY, SO HIS EARS ARE COMPLETELY PLUGGED UP...
HOW CAN THIS GUY USE SOUND TO ATTACK AN EARLESS, ROTATING MEATBALL...?

HE USES SOUND TO ATTACK WITHOUT EVER BEING IN DIRECT CONTACT WITH HIS OPPONENT, BUT...
...THAT'S WHEN HIS ENEMY'S EARS ARE EXPOSED.

THUD
TAP

THUD
HOP HOP

WHAM
HOP

STAB
THERE'S MY TARGET!

MISSED ME! AND NOW, TO GET FREE FROM THERE, YOU'RE GOING TO HAVE TO ROTATE THE OPPOSITE WAY...
...WHICH MEANS THAT, FOR A MOMENT, YOU'LL NEED TO STOP SPINNING ENTIRELY...
KLAK
KLAK
!

MY EARS ARE PLUGGED, SO IT'S USELESS!
!
TAP

NO...
YOU'RE DONE FOR!
PLINK

WAAAH!!

READ THIS WAY

OH!!

FWUMP

OVER 70% OF THE HUMAN BODY IS COMPOSED OF WATER... A GREAT CONDUCTOR OF SOUND. SO IT'S NOT DIFFICULT TO TRANSMIT SHOCK WAVES THROUGH A WALL OF FLESH.
AS LONG AS HE CEASED THOSE VEXING ROTATIONS, I COULD TARGET THE APPROXIMATE LOCATION OF HIS EARDRUMS, AND...

WE HAVE A WINNER!!
DOSU KINUTA!!

LORD OROCHIMARU...
OR RATHER... OROCHIMARU...

I'LL SHOW YOU...
GRIP
...I'M NOT JUST YOUR GUINEA PIG!

HEY, ARE YOU ALL RIGHT?!
I...I WANT...
...TO EAT MEAT...
HE EVEN WENT EASY ON HIM...
WELL... HE LOST, BUT I GUESS I'LL STILL TAKE HIM OUT FOR BARBECUE.
PHEW...
KOFF
KOFF
IT'S FINALLY OVER...

AT LAST...
...THE FINALS...

UH... WELL THEN, AS OF THIS MOMENT, THE PRELIMINARIES TO THE THIRD EXAM...
...ARE NOW COMPLETE!

Number 88:

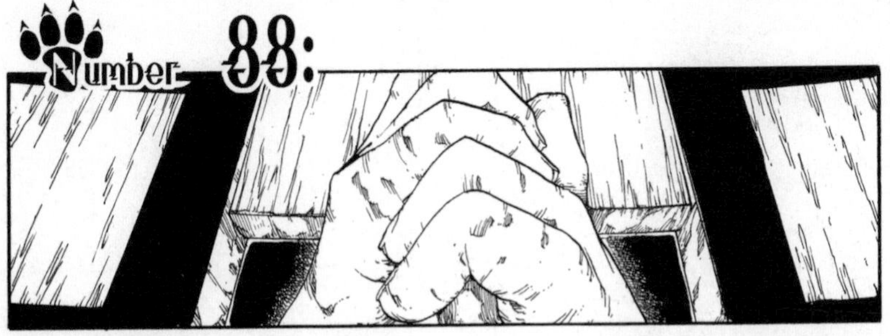

What About Sasuke...?!

TO THOSE OF YOU WHO WON YOUR BOUTS AND QUALIFIED FOR THE FINALS OF THE THIRD PHASE OF THE CHÛNIN EXAM...
... ALTHOUGH ONE OF YOU ISN'T HERE...
KOFF
CONGRATULATIONS!

MASTER KAKASHI...
!

...

READ
THIS
WAY

...I...
I WANT TO ASK YOU SOME-THING...

WELL...
UNFOR-TUNATELY, I DON'T KNOW VERY MUCH YET, EITHER...
BUT... DON'T BE TOO WORRIED.

...SOME-THING ABOUT SASUKE...?

...WHATEVER COMES NEXT...
...IT'S UP TO SASUKE NOW.

...
SAKURA, I'M GOING TO STEP OUT FOR A LITTLE BIT, SO...
...LISTEN CAREFULLY TO THE EXPLANATION OF THE FINALS FOR ME, OKAY...?
HUP
HUH?
UH... OKAY...
VWM

...

INCLUDING THE ABSENT UCHIHA SASUKE, THERE ARE... FIVE KONOHA...
...THREE SAND NINJA... AND ONE SOUND... HMM.

UH... WELL, LORD HOKAGE... THEY'RE ALL YOURS.
YES...

WELL THEN... STARTING NOW...

...I SHALL BEGIN EXPLAINING THE FINALS...

OKAY! FINALLY!!

I WONDER HOW IT TURNED OUT...
...FOR NARUTO...

!

HEY, LET'S SNEAK OUT NOW WHILE WE CAN!
MASTER IRUKA'S BEEN TOTALLY DISTRACTED LATELY, SO THIS IS OUR CHANCE!

BLINK
!

HEY!! KONOHAMARU!!
TRYING TO PLAY HOOKY AGAIN, HUH?
I...I NEED TO USE THE BATHROOM, SIR!!

THE PRE-LIMINARIES HAVE SAFELY CONCLUDED...
...THEY WILL NOW PROCEED TO THE FINALS.

...

READ
THIS
WAY

HOW TRANQUIL... OR RATHER...
CHIRP
CHIRP
...HOW NAIVELY PEACEFUL THIS NATION HAS BECOME...
...WHILE ALL THE OTHER COUNTRIES ARE BUSY WITH MILITARY EXPANSION RACES...

SO IF WE STRIKE NOW...?

...ARE YOU SO SURE OF YOURSELF...?

WELL, YES...
ALTHOUGH I DOUBT IT WOULD BE ANY FUN TO KILL THAT FEEBLE OLD GEEZER...

TO ME...
...IT STILL SEEMS LIKE YOU'RE FALTERING...
...

SOON, THE POWERS OF EACH HIDDEN VILLAGE WILL COLLIDE AND ENTER A FIERCE, LENGTHY CONFLICT...
OTOGAKURE, THE HIDDEN SOUND VILLAGE, WILL BE ONE OF THOSE INVOLVED...
...AND YOU'RE PLANNING TO BE THE TRIGGER OF THAT...

...

AND TO THAT END, THAT BOY...
...HE'S A BULLET, RIGHT?
...UCHIHA SASUKE, WASN'T IT...?

HEH...
YOUR INSIGHTS ARE DISGUSTINGLY ACCURATE...

WELL, OBVIOUSLY NOT...

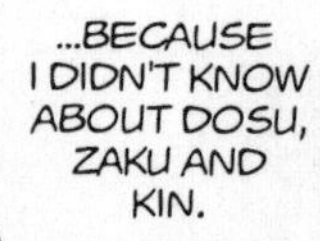
...BECAUSE I DIDN'T KNOW ABOUT DOSU, ZAKU AND KIN.

WHEN I WAS ASSIGNED TO GATHER INTELLIGENCE ON SASUKE...
...I WANTED TO UNDERSTAND THE POWER OF THOSE THREE SOUND NINJA.
I MADE A FOOLISH TACTICAL ERROR... I EVEN PROVOKED THEM INTO ATTACKING ME...
...AND OVER-ESTIMATED MY OWN DEFENSES.

READ THIS WAY

IT SEEMS... YOU STILL DON'T PUT YOUR FULL TRUST IN ME...
...ISN'T THAT RIGHT?

THOSE THREE ARE SO INCONSEQUENTIAL... IS IT REALLY NECESSARY FOR ME TO TELL YOU OF SUCH TRIVIALITIES?
YOU'RE MY RIGHT-HAND MAN... THAT ITSELF IS EVIDENCE OF MY TRUST.

...

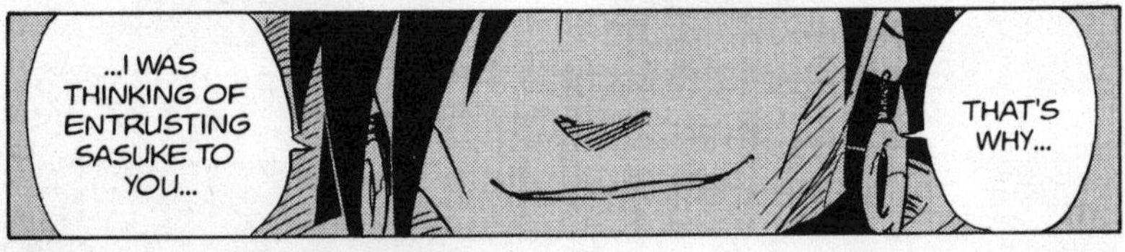
THAT'S WHY...
...I WAS THINKING OF ENTRUSTING SASUKE TO YOU...

THE CURSE MARK I PUT ON HIM... IT SEEMS IT'S BEEN SEALED BY THAT PESKY KAKASHI...
...NOT THAT IT'S OF MUCH CONSEQUENCE.
BUT BEFORE THE DARKNESS IN HIS SOUL IS EXTINGUISHED...

HOW UNLIKE YOU...
YOU'RE WORRIED!

THERE IS SOMETHING CAUSING ME A BIT OF CONCERN...

YOU MEAN... UZUMAKI NARUTO?

...I WANT YOU TO KIDNAP HIM RIGHT AWAY.

AND YET... WHEN WE FOUGHT EACH OTHER... EVEN THOUGH HE KNEW HE COULDN'T PREVAIL AGAINST ME...
...HE CAME AT ME WITHOUT ANY FEAR OF DEATH.
AND I HADN'T THOUGHT HE WAS A CHILD WHO WOULD RUSH SO EAGERLY TO HIS DEMISE...

SASUKE IS AN EMBODIMENT OF VENGEANCE... HIS SOLE REASON FOR LIVING IS THE DESIRE TO KILL HIS OLDER BROTHER.
UNTIL HE ACHIEVES THAT GOAL, HE CANNOT DIE.
HEH... A SHARP CHILD, INDEED...

READ
THIS
WAY

ACCORDING TO YOUR NOTES, IT SEEMS THAT HIS CONTACT WITH THE NINE-TAILED FOX CHILD...
...IS CHANGING SASUKE'S PURPOSE AND HIS SOUL.
FWUP
SINCE NARUTO POSSESSES SO MUCH INFLUENCE OVER SASUKE...
...I MUST SEPARATE THEM IMMEDIATELY...

AS SOON AS I CAN, I'VE GOT TO STAIN HIM WITH MY COLORS...
LICK

SHUDDER

WELL THEN...
TAK
KABUTO... YOU...

IF YOU WANT TO STOP ME...

...YOUR ONLY CHANCE IS TO KILL SASUKE NOW.

!!

EVEN IF YOU'RE STRONG...
YOU'RE NO STRONGER THAN KAKASHI, SO...
THERE'S NO WAY YOU COULD KILL ME, EH?

GULP

HEH... I'M JOKING...

NOW... YOU MAY GO!
I'M PUTTING MY TRUST IN YOU...

...

READ THIS WAY

HOP
VWM

HEH... THAT FACE...
I WONDER WHAT HE'S THINKING...

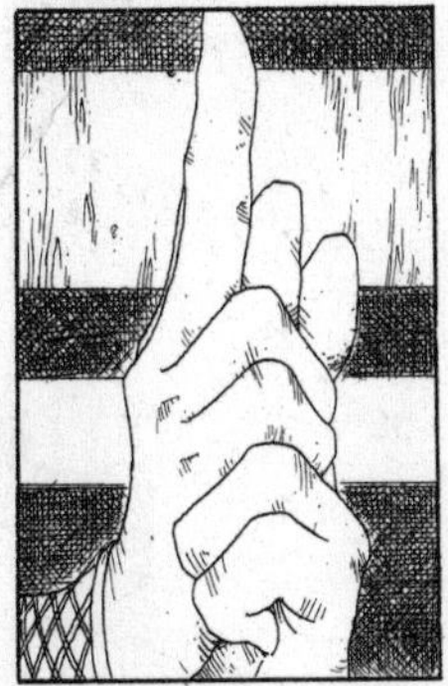

AS I MENTIONED EARLIER, YOU WILL CONDUCT YOUR FINAL ROUND BATTLES IN FRONT OF EVERYONE.
EACH OF YOU REPRESENTS THE BATTLE STRENGTHS OF YOUR RESPECTIVE LANDS...
...SO WE WANT YOU TO EXHIBIT AND FULLY SHOWCASE YOUR VARIOUS TALENTS.

AND THUS THE FINALS...
...WILL COMMENCE ONE MONTH FROM NOW!

!
WE'RE NOT DOING IT RIGHT HERE, RIGHT NOW?

WE CALL THIS THE REQUISITE PREPARATION PERIOD...
WHAT DO YOU MEAN?

WELL...
IT'S A PERIOD OF TIME THAT ALLOWS US TO RELAY THE RESULTS OF THE PRELIMINARIES TO THE RULERS AND SHINOBI LEADERS OF EACH LAND... AND TO SUMMON THEM TO THE FINALS...
...AND IT ALSO SERVES AS A PREPARATION PERIOD FOR YOU APPLICANTS.

THIS OLD GEEZER, HE ALWAYS BEATS AROUND THE BUSH...
I STILL DON'T GET IT! WHAT DO YOU MEAN?

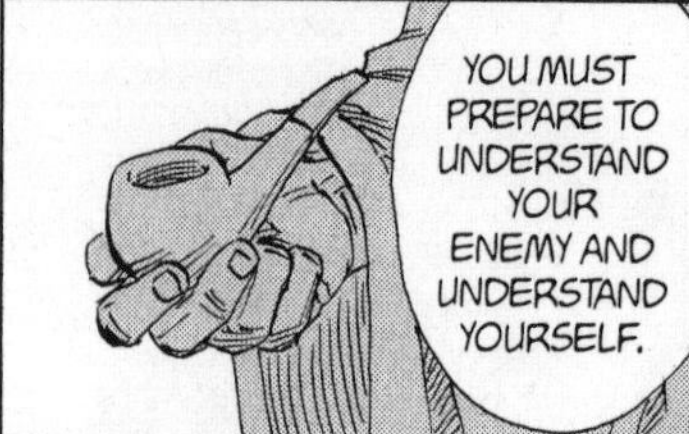
YOU MUST PREPARE TO UNDERSTAND YOUR ENEMY AND UNDERSTAND YOURSELF.

DURING THIS PERIOD, YOU CAN ANALYZE THE INTELLIGENCE YOU HAVE GATHERED ON YOUR FOES DURING THE PRELIMINARIES...
...AND USE IT TO INCREASE YOUR CHANCES OF VICTORY.
EVEN THOUGH, UP TO THIS POINT, ALL THE BATTLES HAVE BEEN REAL BATTLES...
...THEY WERE CONDUCTED ON THE PREMISE THAT YOU WERE FIGHTING AN "UNKNOWN ENEMY"...

...WELL, YEAH...!
I NEVER DREAMED THAT THIS GUY WOULD USE SAND AS A WEAPON...

READ THIS WAY

SOME OF YOU PROBABLY ENDED UP EXPOSING EVERYTHING YOU'VE GOT IN FRONT OF YOUR RIVALS...
...AND SOME OF YOU MAY HAVE GONE UP AGAINST COMPARATIVELY STRONG OPPONENTS AND FOUND YOURSELVES BADLY INJURED.
HOWEVER, THE FINALS ARE A DIFFERENT STORY...

IN ORDER TO MAKE THE FINALS FAIR AND JUST, WE GIVE YOU THIS MONTH.
EACH OF YOU MUST EMBRACE THE OPPORTUNITY TO PRACTICE HARD, LEARN SOME NEW TRICKS...
...AND OF COURSE GET SOME REST, AS WELL!

AT THIS RATE, IT WON'T BE ENOUGH...
JUST ONE MONTH... THERE'S NO WAY I'LL HAVE THE LUXURY OF ANY RELAXATION!

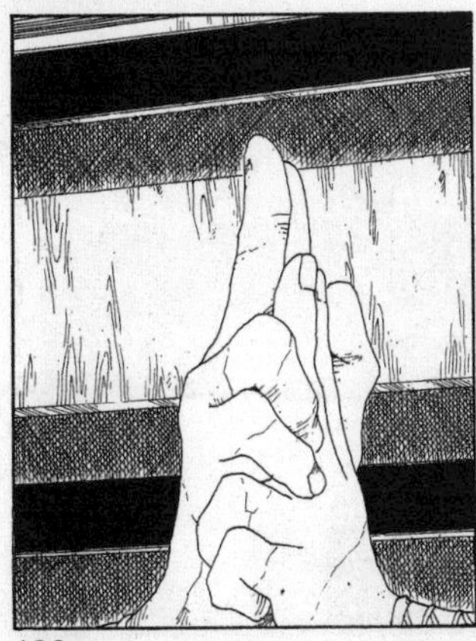

THUD
THUD
THUD

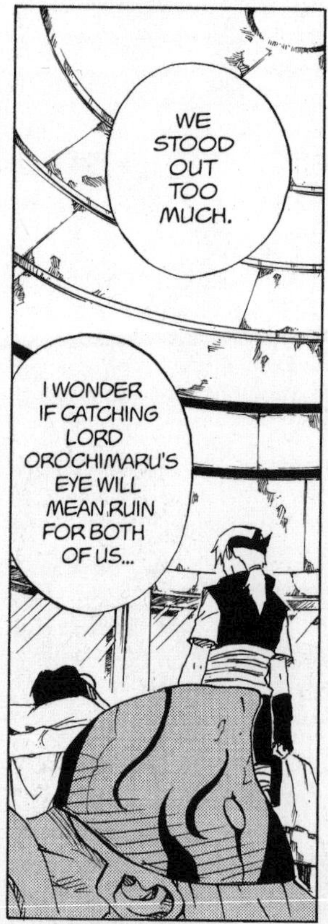
WE STOOD OUT TOO MUCH.
I WONDER IF CATCHING LORD OROCHIMARU'S EYE WILL MEAN RUIN FOR BOTH OF US...

TAK
TAK
SIGH...
AN EXCESS OF BRILLIANCE CAN BE A DISADVANTAGE...

READ
THIS
WAY

HE'S SO YOUNG... HOW COULD HE HAVE THIS DEMON DWELLING IN HIS HEART? IT WILL SERVE HIS PURPOSES NICELY...
...WHEN HE EVENTUALLY USES THAT TECHNIQUE TO MAKE THIS KID INTO...

KABUTO...

PERHAPS YOU REALLY WILL...
...KILL SASUKE, AFTER ALL...

SWUP

SHOOM!!

SNATCH

ONLY YOU, KAKASHI...
...WOULD THINK TO STOP MY ATTACK FROM MY BLIND SPOT...

READ
THIS
WAY

YOU...
YOU'RE NO ORDINARY GENIN, ARE YOU...?

YOU MADE YOUR ATTACK IMMEDIATELY UPON NOTICING MY PRESENCE... YOU'RE PRETTY IMPRESSIVE.

NO...
I'M NOT SO GREAT...

WHAT DO YOU WANT WITH SASUKE?
DEPENDING ON THE CIRCUM-STANCES...
...I'LL HAVE TO ARREST AND INTERROGATE YOU.

I WONDER IF YOU CAN...?

... SOMEONE LIKE YOU...?

TAK

YOU WANT TO TEST "SOMEONE LIKE ME"...?

Number 89: Naruto's Wish...!!

WHAT ARE YOU?!

EVERY SINGLE ONE OF THE BLACK OPS SOLDIERS I HAD GATHERED!..
HE SLAUGHTERED THEM ALL!.. AND WITH SUCH EASE!

YOU'RE... THE SON OF...
...A KONOHA NINJA DOCTOR, RIGHT? A PERPETUAL FAILURE OF A NINJA...
YOUR NAME IS... KABUTO, YES?

...

...NEXT TIME, YOU SHOULD PROBABLY READY...
...AT LEAST 10 GUARDS.

READ THIS WAY

JUST SHUT UP AND ANSWER MY QUESTIONS.

AND WHAT IF I REFUSE?

I'M THE ONE ASKING THE QUESTIONS HERE...
...SHOW SOME RESPECT.
...

ARE YOU...
...IN LEAGUE WITH OROCHIMARU?

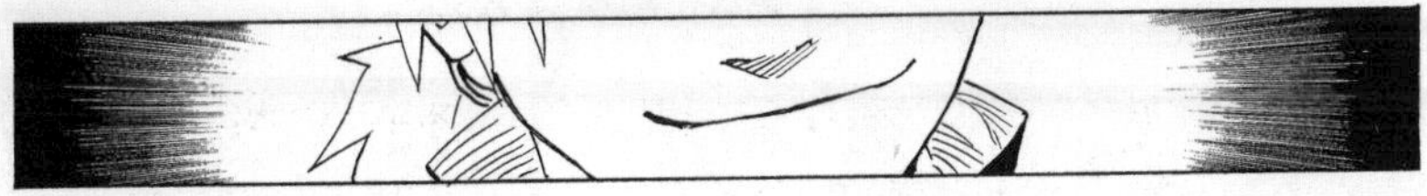

IF YOU ARREST ME HERE, RIGHT NOW, YOU MIGHT NEVER BE ABLE TO PROVE MY CONNECTION TO OROCHIMARU.
NO MATTER WHAT KIND OF TORTURE OR GENJUTSU YOU INFLICT UPON ME, I WON'T SPILL A SINGLE SECRET...
AND BESIDES, I DON'T REALLY LIKE CONFRONTA-TIONS.

IT'LL ALL COME OUT EVENTUALLY, SO...
...WHY DON'T YOU JUST LET IT GO FOR NOW?

YOU... YOU'RE JUST A SELFISH LITTLE BRAT, AREN'T YOU...?

THWP
...YOU SHOULDN'T MOCK YOUR SUPERIORS.

SHF

TWIK
YOU WON'T JUST RELEASE ME, THEN?

YOU KNOW THE LAWS OF THIS VILLAGE...
...HOW SPIES ARE DEALT WITH.
YOU'RE ACTING AWFULLY SMUG, CONSIDERING...
...THAT THE CIRCUMSTANCES ARE IN MY FAVOR...
!

SHF

!
TCH
FWIP!!
CHING
WHAK

HOP
FUMP
TAK

A SHADOW DOPPEL-GANGER!!
SKF

OH... AHA!

!!

TAK
UGH...
BLINK
TAP

THOK
KRAK
KRAK
THOK
THOK
KRAK
THOK
HOP

WOBBLE

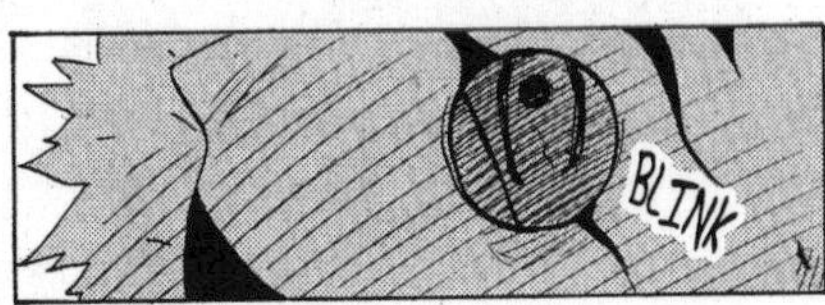
BLINK

!
SLAM

HUP

WHOOSH

SWP

SKF
DARN IT... HE GOT AWAY...

...!

FUMP POOF
AMAZING...

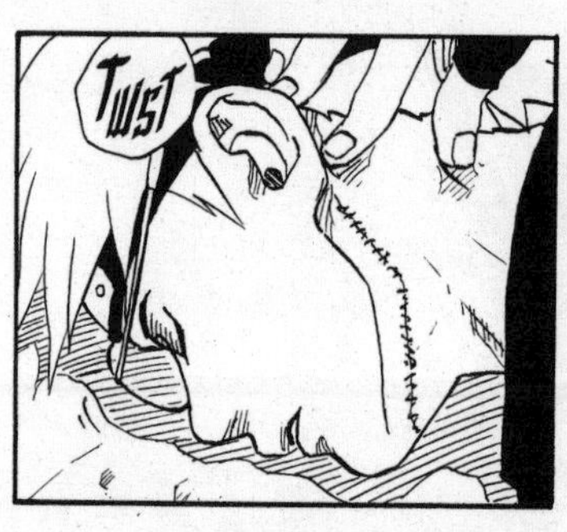
TWST

JUST AS I THOUGHT... *SHIKON NO JUTSU*... THE ART OF DEAD SOULS, USED TO TEMPORARILY RESTORE A CADAVER'S HEART BEAT AND MANIPULATE THE CORPSE...
HE SURGICALLY ALTERED THE FACE... TO MAKE IT RESEMBLE HIS OWN...!
I'M AMAZED... HE WAS SO THOROUGH IN HIS DECEPTION THAT HE EVEN ERASED THE DEAD BODY'S ODOR...
AND HE STILLED HIS OWN HEARTBEAT... DISGUISING HIMSELF AS ONE OF THE BLACK OPS SOLDIERS HE HAD KILLED... TO ALLOW HIS ESCAPE.
THE INFLUENCE OF HIS ADOPTIVE FATHER, THE CHIEF OF THE MEDICAL CORPS, IS OBVIOUS...
...IN THE WAY HE ENJOYS TRIFLING WITH CORPSES...

READ THIS WAY

HIS MOVES WOULD PUT EVEN THE UNDERTAKER SQUAD TO SHAME...
IF SUCH A TALENTED PERSON IS WORKING UNDER OROCHIMARU, THEN...
AT THIS RATE, I'LL BE OBSOLETE SOON, TOO...

SO... THOSE ARE THE BASICS.

I WOULD LIKE TO LET YOU ALL GO NOW, BUT FIRST...
...THERE'S ONE LAST THING WE MUST DO FOR THE FINALS.

HEY, COME ON!
I NEED TO START TRAINING NOW!!

NOW THEN, DON'T BE SO IM-PATIENT...
THERE ARE SLIPS OF PAPER INSIDE THE BOX ANKO IS HOLDING... EACH OF YOU, TAKE ONE.
I'LL COME AROUND, SO LINE UP, OKAY?

ONE PER PERSON!
DIG DIG
LUB DUP

TUG

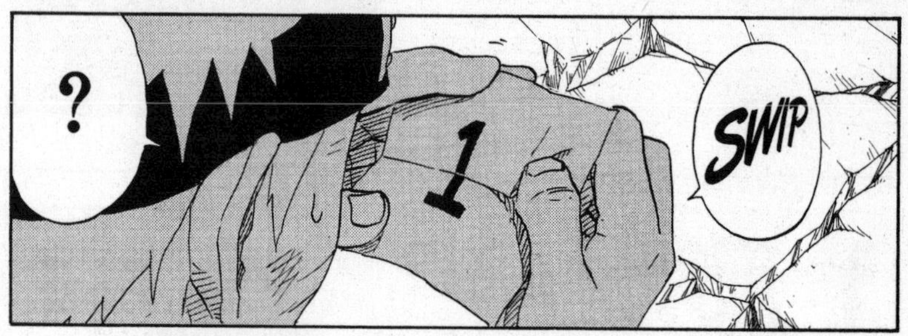
SWIP
?
1

ALL RIGHT... DOES EVERYBODY HAVE ONE NOW...?
THEN... STARTING AT THE LEFT, EACH OF YOU READ OUT THE NUMBER WRITTEN ON YOUR SLIP!

5

7

I GOT 1!

I HAVE 8.

READ THIS WAY

3

9

2

6

SO UCHIHA WILL BE NUMBER 4...
GOOD!

AND NOW I WILL REVEAL...
...THE MATCH ORDER FOR THE TOURNAMENT-STYLE FINALS!!

WHAT?!
SO THAT'S WHAT THE DRAWING WAS FOR?!

WELL, IBIKI, SHOW THEM THE PAIRINGS.
YES SIR...

GULP

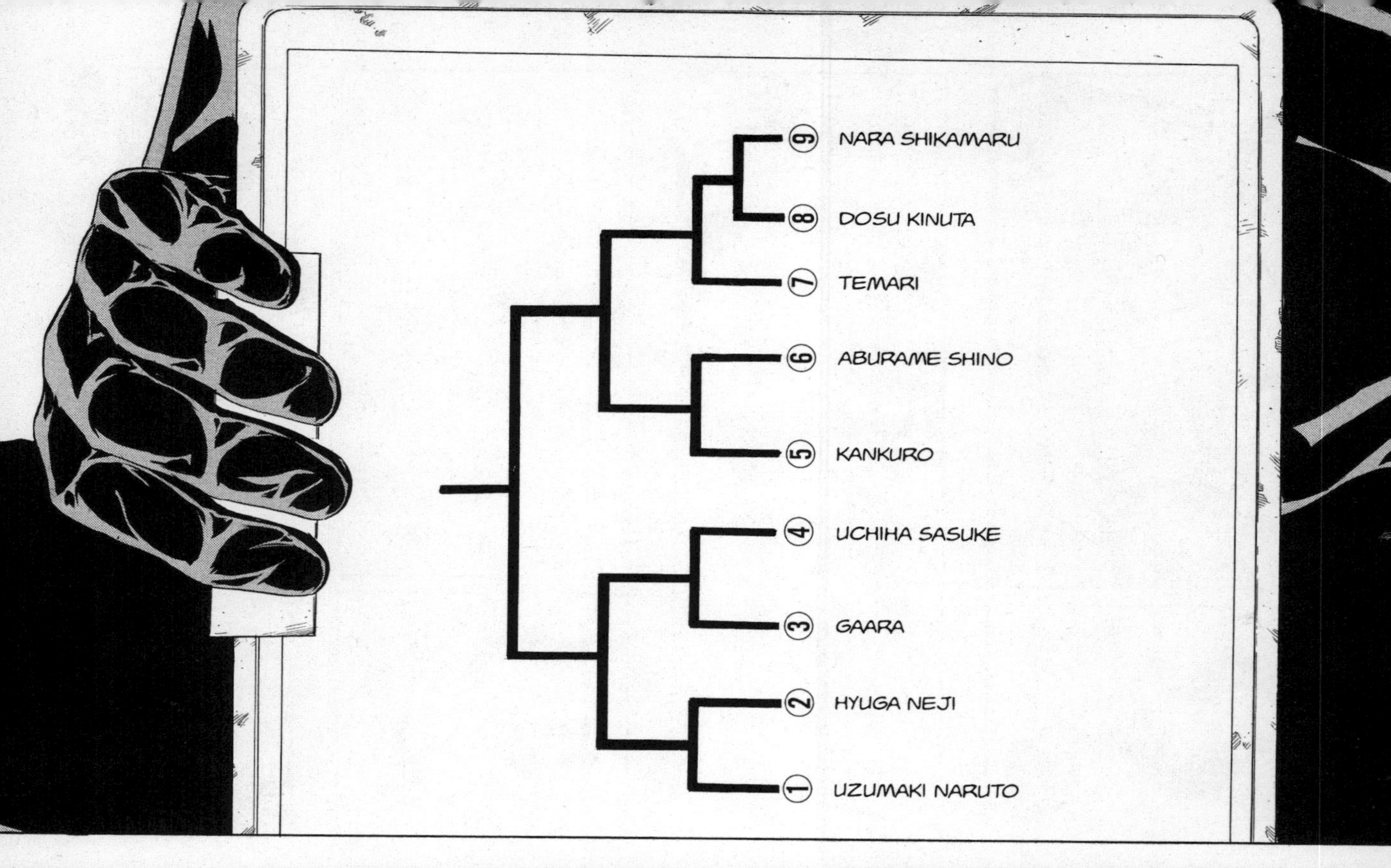
① UZUMAKI NARUTO
② HYUGA NEJI
③ GAARA
④ UCHIHA SASUKE
⑤ KANKURO
⑥ ABURAME SHINO
⑦ TEMARI
⑧ DOSU KINUTA
⑨ NARA SHIKAMARU

READ
THIS
WAY

...

MY MATCH COMES LATE IN THE GAME...

WHAT?
THE FINALS ARE A SIMPLE TOURNAMENT...?

MAN, I'VE GOT TO FIGHT AN EXTRA ROUND.
AND I DON'T WANT TO HAVE TO AVENGE CHOJI...
NO THANKS!

SIGH...
I'M IN A DIFFERENT BRACKET THAN GAARA...
THANK GOODNESS.

UCHIHA... SASUKE...

...PERFECT.

HYUGA NEJI, RIGHT OFF THE BAT?

I NEVER DREAMED OF A BETTER OPPONENT!

NOW THEN... IT'S TIME FOR YOU TO GO PLAN YOUR STRATEGIES, REST UP, OR WHATEVER YOU PLEASE.
WE'RE ALL FINISHED HERE... UNLESS ANY OF YOU HAVE QUESTIONS?
MAY I?
SURE!

YOU SAID THIS IS A TOURNAMENT, SO...
...THERE'S ONLY ONE WINNER, RIGHT...?
THEN... DOES THAT MEAN ONLY ONE PERSON GETS TO BECOME A CHÛNIN?

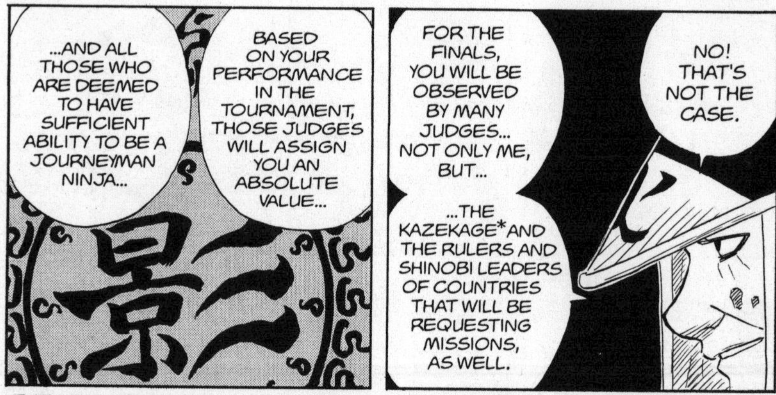
NO! THAT'S NOT THE CASE.
FOR THE FINALS, YOU WILL BE OBSERVED BY MANY JUDGES... NOT ONLY ME, BUT...
...THE KAZEKAGE* AND THE RULERS AND SHINOBI LEADERS OF COUNTRIES THAT WILL BE REQUESTING MISSIONS, AS WELL.
BASED ON YOUR PERFORMANCE IN THE TOURNAMENT, THOSE JUDGES WILL ASSIGN YOU AN ABSOLUTE VALUE...
...AND ALL THOSE WHO ARE DEEMED TO HAVE SUFFICIENT ABILITY TO BE A JOURNEYMAN NINJA...

*THE LEADER OF THE VILLAGE OF SUNAGAKURE (THE VILLAGE HIDDEN IN SAND).

DO YOU MEAN...
...IT'S POSSIBLE THAT ALL OF US HERE COULD BECOME CHÛNIN?

YES.

...EVEN THOSE WHO MAY HAVE LOST IN THE FIRST ROUND...
...CAN BECOME CHÛNIN.

READ THIS WAY

HOWEVER, IT IS ALSO POSSIBLE...
...THAT NONE OF YOU WILL BECOME CHÛNIN!

DOES THAT ANSWER YOUR QUESTION, SHIKAMARU?!
GEEZ... HE DIDN'T HAVE TO THROW IT BACK IN MY FACE...

THE ADVANTAGE OF FIGHTING IN MORE ROUNDS IN THE TOURNAMENT...
...IS IN HAVING A GREATER NUMBER OF OPPORTUNITIES TO DISPLAY YOUR TALENTS FOR THE JUDGES.

WELL THEN, GOOD WORK, ALL!
YOU ARE DISMISSED UNTIL ONE MONTH FROM NOW!

MY SECOND ROUND WILL BE AGAINST EITHER THAT BROWLESS SAND GUY OR SASUKE...?

HE WAS STRONG ENOUGH TO WIPE THE FLOOR WITH BUSHY BROWS, SO...

NARUTO...
YOU'RE ONE OF THE ONES I WANT TO FIGHT...

...
I'D BETTER ASK MASTER KAKASHI FOR HELP!

SASUKE... AGAINST THAT GUY...

SAKURA!! WHERE'S MASTER KAKASHI?!
!

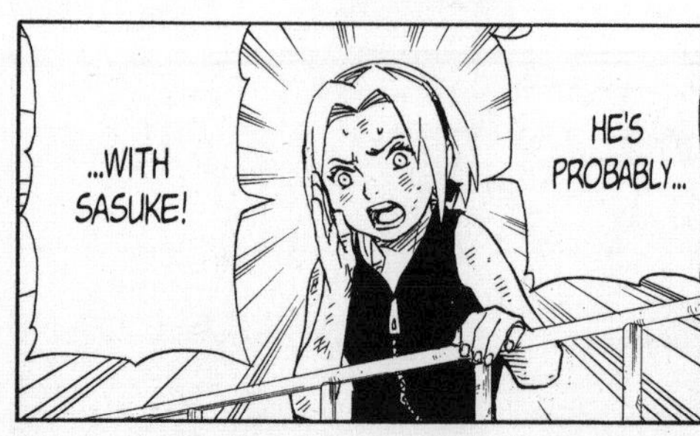
HE'S PROBABLY...
...WITH SASUKE!

THANKS, SAKURA!

...

READ
THIS
WAY

HOSPITAL
KONOHA
HEY! WHERE'S SASUKE'S HOSPITAL ROOM?!
VISITING HOURS ARE OVER.
BUT... WHY?!
SORRY... HOSPITAL POLICY.

NARUTO, YOU'RE IN A HOSPITAL! BE QUIET!

OH! MASTER KAKASHI!!

HEY! I NEED A FAVOR!
TAK TAK
STOP RIGHT THERE... I ALREADY KNOW WHAT YOU'RE ABOUT TO ASK, SO...

I'VE FOUND SOMEONE TO OVERSEE YOUR TRAINING.
HUH?!
I WANT YOU TO TRAIN ME, MASTER KAKASHI!

I'VE GOT OTHER THINGS GOING ON...
...I COULDN'T GIVE YOU MY FULL ATTENTION.

HMPH!
...

LET ME GUESS! YOU'RE TRAINING SASUKE, RIGHT?!
STAB
NOW, NOW! DON'T COMPLAIN.
I FOUND YOU AN EVEN BETTER TEACHER THAN ME.

WHO IS IT?!
IT IS I!!

!
HUH?
YOU'RE... HEY!

...SUPER-PERV!!
HOW RUDE!
POKE

THE WORLD OF KISHIMOTO MASASHI
MY PERSONAL HISTORY, PART 13

ONCE I WAS EXPOSED TO *AKIRA*, MY ATTITUDE TOWARD ART BEGAN TO CHANGE DRAMATICALLY. I DID SOME RESEARCH ON THE STYLE OF MR. OTOMO, THE AUTHOR AND ARTIST OF *AKIRA*, IN AN ATTEMPT TO LEARN WHICH ARTISTS HAD INFLUENCED HIM... BUT I COULDN'T FIND ANYTHING. SO I CONCLUDED THAT IT WAS COMPLETELY ORIGINAL... AND THAT'S WHEN IT CAME TO ME: "WOW, THIS IS THE FIRST TIME SINCE SEEING MR. TORIYAMA'S WORK THAT I'VE BEEN SO STRONGLY AFFECTED BY SOMEONE'S ART."

I HAD ABSOLUTELY NO IDEA WHY MR. TORIYAMA'S AND MR. OTOMO'S ART WERE BOTH SO FASCINATING, BUT THERE WERE TWO THINGS THAT I WAS SURE OF. BOTH OF THEM DID WORK THAT SEEMED ORIGINAL AND HAD A GREAT SENSE OF STYLE. I HAD THE FEELING THAT THEIR EFFECTS, DESIGN AND ATTENTION TO DETAIL WERE TOTALLY DIFFERENT FROM THOSE OF OTHER PEOPLE. IN OTHER WORDS, I STARTED THINKING THAT WHAT "FASCINATING ART" MEANT TO ME WAS "ORIGINAL ART," AND THAT COPYCAT ART, NO MATTER HOW TECHNICALLY SKILLFUL, WAS MEANINGLESS.

AFTER THAT, I TRIED TO MAKE SURE THAT EVERYTHING I DREW WAS TRULY ORIGINAL... BUT I ALWAYS ENDED UP LETTING OUTSIDE INFLUENCES CREEP IN, AND MY END PRODUCT WASN'T ORIGINAL AFTER ALL. STILL UNSATISFIED WITH MY RESULTS, I BEGAN STUDYING THE WORK OF MANY DIFFERENT MANGA ARTISTS, ONE BY ONE, WONDERING IF I COULD FIND ANY OTHERS WHOSE ART COULD RIVAL THAT OF THE TWO I ALREADY REVERED.

THAT'S WHEN I REALIZED THAT THE ARTISTS WHOSE WORK I FOUND INTERESTING WERE ALL INFLUENCED EITHER BY ONE OR BOTH OF THE ABOVE TWO, OR BY SOMEONE ELSE, AND THAT A TOTALLY ORIGINAL STYLE IS VERY RARE. IN ANY CASE, I THOUGHT MR. OTOMO HAD THE BEST STYLE OF THEM ALL, SO I STARTED IMITATING HIM. IN THE BEGINNING OF EIGHTH OR NINTH GRADE, I BOUGHT ALL THE *AKIRA*-RELATED MATERIALS I COULD FIND -- THE ART BOOK, MANGA AND MOVIE MANGA -- AND FURIOUSLY COPIED THEM. BUT I CONTINUED TO STRIVE FOR MY OWN STYLE AND WORKED HARD AT ALL DIFFERENT SORTS OF ORIGINAL ART AS WELL. (LATER, I WOULD ENCOUNTER TWO OTHER ARTISTS WHOM I CAME TO CONSIDER ORIGINAL AND STYLISH, BUT THAT IS A TALE FOR ANOTHER DAY.)

Number 90:

What About My Training?!

MASTER EBISU...
...A SUPER-PERV?

WHY WOULD YOU CHOOSE SUCH A LOSER TO BE MY TRAINER?!
?
BESIDES, THIS GUY IS EVEN WEAKER THAN ME!

COME ON! I MEAN, ONE TIME HE EVEN FELL FOR MY NINJA HAREM TECHNIQUE, AND HE...
HEY!
!!
D...DON'T SAY IT!!

SMOOCH
CLAMP
MMPH!

NINJA HAREM ...?
UH...UM... IT'S NOTHING, SIR! HA HA...

I'LL TREAT YOU TO WHATEVER YOU WANT LATER, SO...
...DON'T SAY ANYTHING MORE ABOUT IT, OK?!
...SWEAR ON IT!

...WOW, I DIDN'T KNOW YOU TWO KNEW EACH OTHER...

I SHALL NEVER FORGET THAT HUMILIATION...
HA HA... WELL, MAYBE OPPOSITES ATTRACT, OR...
RIGHT?!
PAT PAT
BUT... WHY HIM?!
THIS STINKS...

INDEED! IF IT WEREN'T FOR KAKASHI'S REQUEST...

...I WOULD NEVER CHOOSE TO TEACH YOU!

GRR!!

HEY! BOTH OF YOU... PLEASE...

NARUTO! MASTER EBISU IS AN EXCLUSIVE PRIVATE TUTOR WHO TEACHES THE ELITE... HE'S A SPECIAL JÔNIN!

HE'S A BETTER TEACHER THAN ME, I PROMISE!

AND, WELL... NARUTO, AMONG THE THREE GENIN IN CELL SEVEN...

...YOU'RE THE WEAKEST AT THE BASICS.

THIS TIME, LISTEN CLOSELY AND LEARN IT RIGHT.

WHOA THERE! COMPARED TO SAKURA AND SASUKE...

...HOW IN THE WORLD DO I COME UP SHORT?!

READ THIS WAY

...
SIGH...
SHRUG

NOD

NARUTO... UPON OBTAINING YOUR INFORMATION FROM MASTER KAKASHI...
...AND CONDUCTING MY ANALYSIS...
...I BELIEVE THAT YOUR CHAKRA CONTROL IS SORELY IN NEED OF IMPROVE-MENT.
SHF

HERE, LET ME EXPLAIN WITH A SERIES OF SIMPLE DIAGRAMS.
POOF
PLEASE, TAKE A LOOK.
?!

THESE SHOW, IN EASY TERMS, THE FLOW OF PHYSICAL AND MENTAL ENERGIES -- COLLECTIVELY CALLED "STAMINA"...

...WHICH MOVE WITHIN THE BODY WHENEVER A NINJA USES NINJUTSU, TAIJUTSU OR GENJUTSU.

THIS DIAGRAM REPRESENTS THE HEALTHY STATE OF FULL STAMINA...

...PRIOR TO USE OF A TECHNIQUE.

I ATE MY RAMEN! AND I SLEPT WELL! I'M AT FULL POWER!!!

TAIJUTSU

STAMINA {MENTAL ENERGY / PHYSICAL ENERGY}

100 %

THE MIXING OF MENTAL AND PHYSICAL ENERGIES OR, IN OTHER WORDS, THE PRODUCTION OF CHAKRA

SIGNS

NINJUTSU OR GENJUTSU

CHAKRA

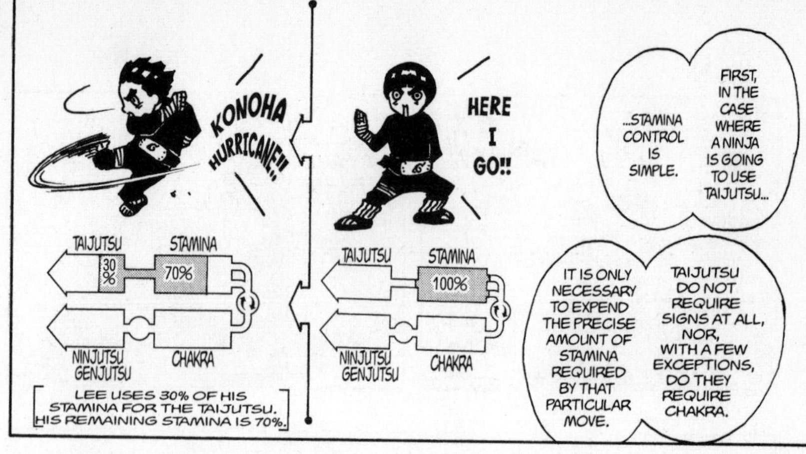
FIRST, IN THE CASE WHERE A NINJA IS GOING TO USE TAIJUTSU...
...STAMINA CONTROL IS SIMPLE.
TAIJUTSU DO NOT REQUIRE SIGNS AT ALL, NOR, WITH A FEW EXCEPTIONS, DO THEY REQUIRE CHAKRA.
IT IS ONLY NECESSARY TO EXPEND THE PRECISE AMOUNT OF STAMINA REQUIRED BY THAT PARTICULAR MOVE.
HERE I GO!!
TAIJUTSU
STAMINA
100%
NINJUTSU GENJUTSU
CHAKRA
KONOHA HURRICANE!!
TAIJUTSU
STAMINA
30%
70%
NINJUTSU GENJUTSU
CHAKRA
LEE USES 30% OF HIS STAMINA FOR THE TAIJUTSU. HIS REMAINING STAMINA IS 70%.

HOWEVER, IN THE CASE OF NINJUTSU OR GENJUTSU...
...ONE MUST FIRST AMASS THE AMOUNT OF CHAKRA REQUIRED TO PERFORM THE PARTICULAR TECHNIQUE!
HUP
I'M GOING TO MAKE CHAKRA!
TAIJUTSU
STAMINA
100%
SIGNS
NINJUTSU GENJUTSU
CHAKRA
HRMMM!!
TAIJUTSU
STAMINA
70%
PRODUCING CHAKRA
SIGNS
30%
NINJUTSU GENJUTSU
CHAKRA
NARUTO HAS CONTRIBUTED 30% OF HIS STAMINA TO THE CREATION OF CHAKRA. 70% OF HIS STAMINA REMAINS.

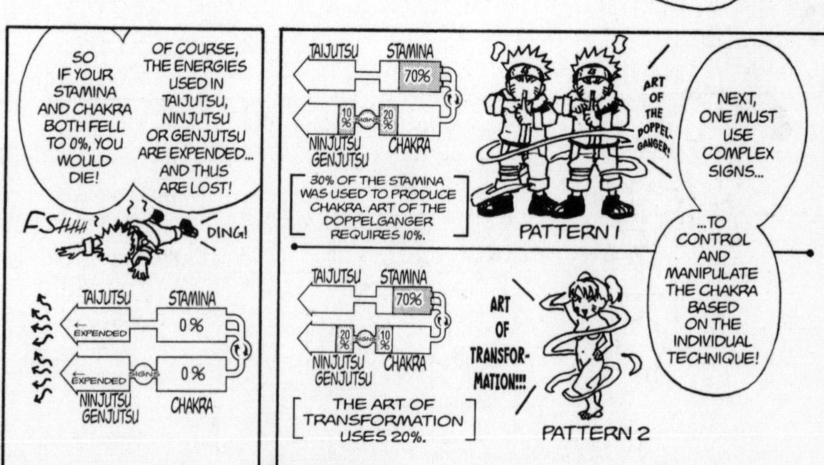
NEXT, ONE MUST USE COMPLEX SIGNS...
...TO CONTROL AND MANIPULATE THE CHAKRA BASED ON THE INDIVIDUAL TECHNIQUE!
ART OF THE DOPPELGANGER!
PATTERN 1
TAIJUTSU
STAMINA
70%
10%
SIGNS
20%
NINJUTSU GENJUTSU
CHAKRA
30% OF THE STAMINA WAS USED TO PRODUCE CHAKRA. ART OF THE DOPPELGANGER REQUIRES 10%.
ART OF TRANSFORMATION!!!
PATTERN 2
TAIJUTSU
STAMINA
70%
20%
SIGNS
10%
NINJUTSU GENJUTSU
CHAKRA
THE ART OF TRANSFORMATION USES 20%.
OF COURSE, THE ENERGIES USED IN TAIJUTSU, NINJUTSU OR GENJUTSU ARE EXPENDED... AND THUS ARE LOST!
SO IF YOUR STAMINA AND CHAKRA BOTH FELL TO 0%, YOU WOULD DIE!
FSHHH
DING!
TAIJUTSU
STAMINA
EXPENDED
0%
EXPENDED
SIGNS
0%
NINJUTSU GENJUTSU
CHAKRA

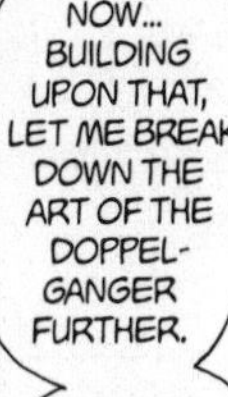

NOW... BUILDING UPON THAT, LET ME BREAK DOWN THE ART OF THE DOPPEL-GANGER FURTHER.
LET'S SAY 30% OF YOUR CHAKRA IS NEEDED TO CREATE THREE DOPPEL-GANGERS.
FWIP

FIRST, IN SAKURA'S CASE, WHEN SHE INITIATES THIS TECHNIQUE, SHE IS ABLE TO CONVERT PRECISELY 30% OF HER STAMINA INTO CHAKRA.
HUP
EASY!

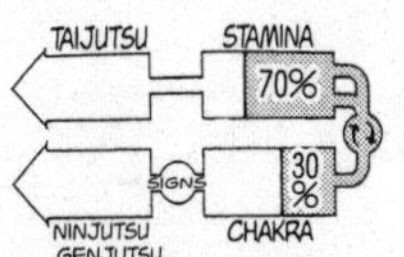
TAIJUTSU
STAMINA
70%
SIGNS
30%
NINJUTSU
GENJUTSU
CHAKRA
[SHE CONVERTS EXACTLY 30%]

THEN, BECAUSE SHE CAN EXPERTLY CONTROL HER CHAKRA VOLUME AS WELL, WHEN SHE BEGINS MAKING HAND SIGNS...
HYAH!!
FWUP
FWUP
ART OF THE DOPPEL-GANGER!
TAIJUTSU
STAMINA
70%
30%
SIGNS
NINJUTSU
GENJUTSU
CHAKRA
[SHE USES EXACTLY 30%]

...SHE CAN CLEANLY PRODUCE THREE COPIES OF HERSELF... AND STILL HAVE 70% OF HER STAMINA LEFT FOR LATER USE!
THREE DOPPELGANGERS!

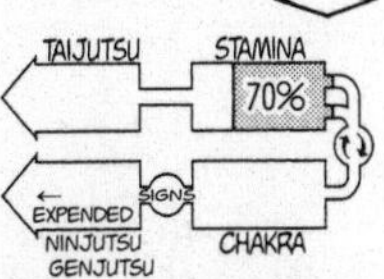
TAIJUTSU
STAMINA
70%
SIGNS
←
EXPENDED
NINJUTSU
GENJUTSU
CHAKRA

NEXT... IN SASUKE'S CASE...

HE KEEPS DRONING ON AND ON... AND I DON'T UNDERSTAND A BIT OF IT...
YEP! OKAY!

HE'S NOT AS EFFICIENT AT CREATING CHAKRA, SO ALTHOUGH HE ONLY NEEDS 30%, HE PRODUCES 40%, OR 10% MORE THAN REQUIRED.
HM!

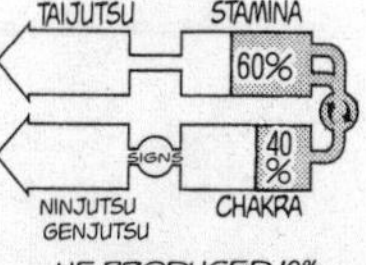
TAIJUTSU
STAMINA
60%
SIGNS
40%
NINJUTSU
GENJUTSU
CHAKRA
[HE PRODUCED 10% MORE THAN NECESSARY]

HOWEVER, HIS CHAKRA CONTROL THROUGH THE USE OF SIGNS IS JUST AS SKILLED AS SAKURA'S, SO... NO PROBLEMS THERE...
ART OF THE DOPPEL-GANGER!
FWUP
FWUP
TAIJUTSU
STAMINA
60%
30%
SIGNS
10%
NINJUTSU
GENJUTSU
CHAKRA
[HERE, HE'S JUST AS GOOD AS SAKURA]

AND HE CAN ALSO CREATE THREE OF HIMSELF, BUT... SINCE SASUKE CANNOT USE OR RECYCLE THE SURPLUS CHAKRA BACK INTO HIS STAMINA POOL, THAT EXTRA 10% GOES TO WASTE... AND HE ONLY HAS 60% OF HIS STAMINA LEFT IN RESERVE!
HMPH

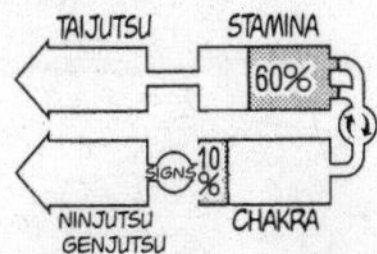
TAIJUTSU
STAMINA
60%
SIGNS
10%
NINJUTSU
GENJUTSU
CHAKRA
[THE REMAINING STAMINA IS AT 60%... AND THE EXTRA CHAKRA IS WASTED]

AHA! SO SASUKE'S NOT SO GREAT AFTER ALL! HA HA!
WELL... YOU'RE IN NO POSITION TO BE LAUGHING AT HIM!

YOU ARE EVEN WORSE THAN SASUKE AT MANIPULATING CHAKRA, SO YOU END UP PRODUCING 50% INSTEAD OF THE REQUIRED 30%.

RRROAR!!

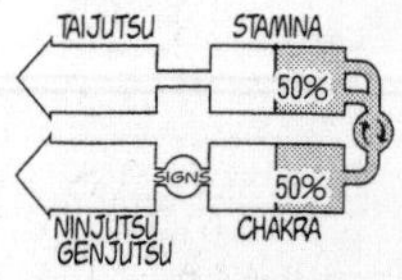
TAIJUTSU
STAMINA
50%
SIGNS
50%
NINJUTSU GENJUTSU
CHAKRA

[PRODUCES 20% MORE THAN NECESSARY]

AND FURTHERMORE, YOUR CHAKRA CONTROL FOR INITIATING TECHNIQUES THROUGH SIGNS IS SO POOR THAT YOU CAN ONLY USE 10% INSTEAD OF THE NECESSARY 30%...

ART OF THE DOPPEL-GANGER!

FWUP

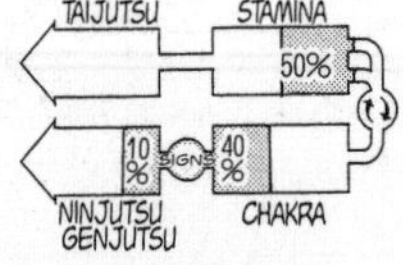
TAIJUTSU
STAMINA
50%
10%
SIGNS
40%
NINJUTSU GENJUTSU
CHAKRA

[30% IS THE FUNDAMENTALLY REQUIRED AMOUNT]

SO YOU END UP WITH ONLY 50% LEFT IN RESERVE, WASTE 40% AND BARELY CREATE A SINGLE DOPPELGANGER! THIS IS HOW DIFFERENT THE THREE OF YOU ARE JUST COMPARING THE SAME TECHNIQUE!

HUH?
HUF
PUF
PUF
HUF

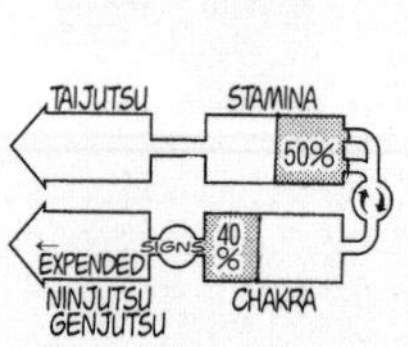
TAIJUTSU
STAMINA
50%
EXPENDED
SIGNS
40%
NINJUTSU GENJUTSU
CHAKRA

[STAMINA REMAINING = 50%
WASTED CHAKRA = 40%.]

WELL, THIS SHOWS THE DIFFERENCES BETWEEN YOU THREE IN A SLIGHTLY EXAGGERATED WAY, BUT...
NARUTO, YOU PRODUCE TOO MUCH CHAKRA AND THUS EXPEND TOO MUCH ENERGY...
AND YOUR TECHNIQUE INITIATION IS ALSO UNSTABLE.

BUT... BUT THERE'VE BEEN TIMES WHEN...
...I WAS WAY BETTER THAN SAKURA OR SASUKE...!
STAB

READ THIS WAY

WHY DID WE COME HERE, THEN?!
ARE WE GONNA TAKE A BATH BEFORE TRAINING?

NO!
THESE HOT SPRINGS ARE WHERE WE SHALL TRAIN!!

?

NOW... HERE WE ARE!
WE'RE GOING TO TRAIN HERE?
WHAT THE HECK ARE WE GOING TO DO?
RUMBLE

HA HA...
?

WE'RE GOING TO...
...WALK ON WATER!

HUH?!

MASTER KAKASHI TOLD ME THAT YOU'D ALREADY MASTERED THE NO-HANDS TREE CLIMBING EXERCISE.
THIS TAKES IT TO THE NEXT LEVEL!

WHAT...?
I MEAN, I DON'T REALLY REMEMBER MUCH FROM WAY BACK THEN!

FOR TREE CLIMBING, YOU ONLY NEED TO GATHER A REQUISITE AMOUNT OF CHAKRA IN THE REQUISITE PLACE...
...AND JUST MAINTAIN THAT SET VOLUME OF CHAKRA THE WHOLE TIME.
FIXED CHAKRA
BECAUSE THE TREE IS A STATIONARY OBJECT, ALL YOU HAVE TO DO IS KEEP YOUR FOOT ATTACHED LIKE A SUCTION CUP...
IT'S AN EXERCISE THAT DEMONSTRATES HOW TO PRODUCE AND MAINTAIN A SET AMOUNT OF CHAKRA.

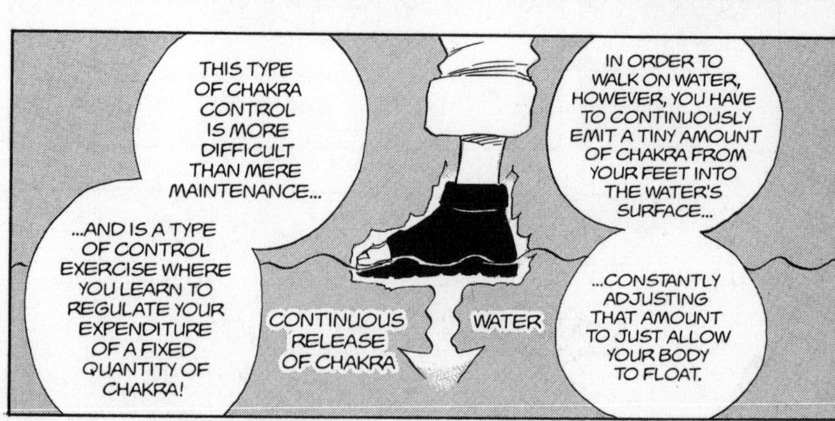
IN ORDER TO WALK ON WATER, HOWEVER, YOU HAVE TO CONTINUOUSLY EMIT A TINY AMOUNT OF CHAKRA FROM YOUR FEET INTO THE WATER'S SURFACE...
...CONSTANTLY ADJUSTING THAT AMOUNT TO JUST ALLOW YOUR BODY TO FLOAT.
WATER
CONTINUOUS RELEASE OF CHAKRA
THIS TYPE OF CHAKRA CONTROL IS MORE DIFFICULT THAN MERE MAINTENANCE...
...AND IS A TYPE OF CONTROL EXERCISE WHERE YOU LEARN TO REGULATE YOUR EXPENDITURE OF A FIXED QUANTITY OF CHAKRA!

HMM... I DON'T GET IT!
SHF
WELL... IT'S PROBABLY EASIER TO JUST SHOW YOU...

FIRST, YOU GATHER CHAKRA TO THE SOLES OF YOUR FEET.
BZZ
ZZ

THEN, WHILE YOU CONTINU-OUSLY EMIT A SET AMOUNT...
...YOU FINE-TUNE IT TO YOUR BODY WEIGHT...
SWP
SPLASH

WHOA!
SPLISH
SPLISH

ALL RIGHT, I WANT TO TRY IT!
FIRST, CHAKRA TO MY SOLES!
BZZ
ZZ

AND THEN RELEASE A SET AMOUNT...!
SWP
SPLASH

SPLOOSH
JUST AS I EXPECTED...

GASP!
HOT! HOT!! HOT!!!

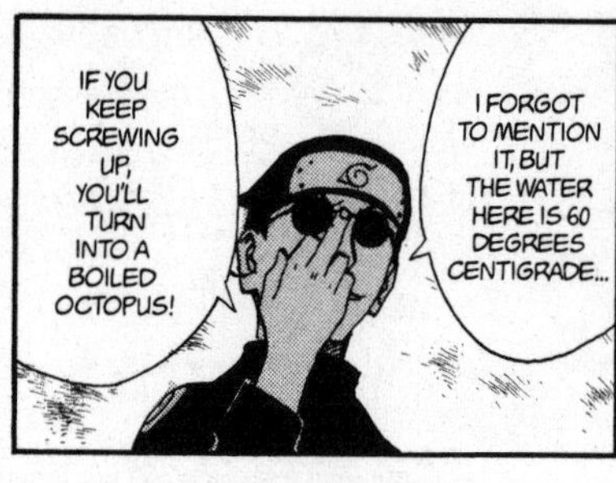
I FORGOT TO MENTION IT, BUT THE WATER HERE IS 60 DEGREES CENTIGRADE...
IF YOU KEEP SCREWING UP, YOU'LL TURN INTO A BOILED OCTOPUS!

HSSS
...AW, MAN!
(HUF)
(HUF)

I CAN DO THIS!!
FWUP

SPLOOSH
OW OW OWWW!

HEH...

YOU'RE UNUSUALLY DILIGENT TODAY, HONORABLE GRANDSON!

NORMALLY, THIS IS THE TIME OF DAY WHEN YOU GO MAKE SURPRISE ATTACKS ON LORD HOKAGE.
I SEE MY TEACHING PRINCIPLES HAVE FINALLY SUNK IN!

I'VE DECIDED TO STOP DOING THAT STUFF...

OH REALLY! YOU FINALLY UNDER-STAND...
...DOING AS I TELL YOU IS THE NUMBER ONE SHORTCUT TO BECOMING HOKAGE!

THERE AIN'T NO SHORTCUT!
HUF
HUF

!
HM?

THAT'S WHAT NARUTO SAID.
...
SKF

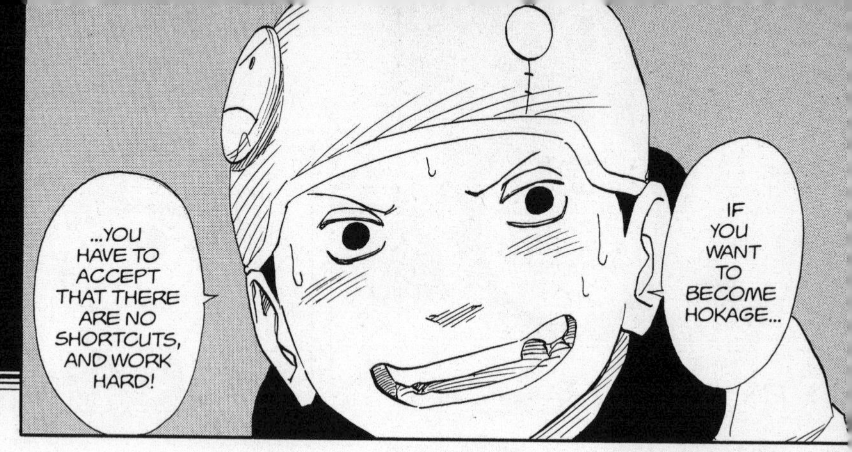
IF YOU WANT TO BECOME HOKAGE...
...YOU HAVE TO ACCEPT THAT THERE ARE NO SHORTCUTS, AND WORK HARD!

HEY!
SLOSH
I THINK I'M STARTING TO GET IT!
SLOSH
SPLISH
SPLISH

...

MY GOODNESS... HE'S GOTTEN THE KNACK OF THIS CHAKRA CONTROL EXERCISE SO QUICKLY...
...I NEVER IMAGINED HE WOULD HAVE MATURED THIS MUCH.

IT SEEMS I HAD UNDER-ESTIMATED YOU...
YOU ARE AN EVEN WISER TEACHER THAN I, AND...
...YOU ARE ALSO MORE THAN JUST A FOX DEMON...

AND IT'S TRUE... NO MATTER THE CONTEXT...
WHOA!
SLOSH
SPLISH
...THERE ARE NO SHORT-CUTS IN LIFE.

READ
THIS
WAY

...YOU ARE TRULY...
...A SPLENDID KONOHA NINJA!
SLOSH

OH--!

SPLOOSH
WAAH!!
!

HEH HEH HEH...

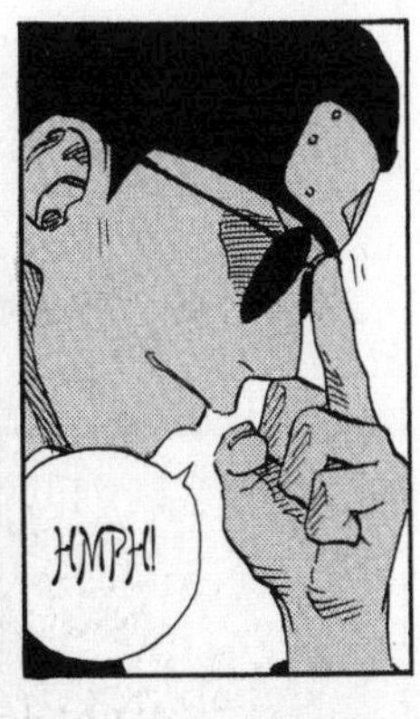
HMPH!

I DON'T KNOW WHO YOU ARE OR WHERE YOU'RE FROM, BUT...
SHOVE

...I WILL NOT PERMIT ANY DISREPUT-ABLE BEHAVIOR!!
HUH?
TAK

SHEESH...
忠
Y... YOU'RE ...!!
SNAP
SPLAT
AARGH!
SMAK

HISSSS
SLURP

YOU'LL GET US BUSTED... AND WHAT'LL WE DO THEN?!
DON'T MAKE A FUSS, EH...? SHEESH.
WH...WHAT'S GOING ON? WHO THE HECK IS THIS BLATANT PERV?!
HE BEAT SUPER-PERV?
...

TO BE CONTINUED IN NARUTO VOL. 11!

IN THE NEXT VOLUME...

A new mentor with rather *unconventional* methods guides Naruto's training — and helps Naruto learn how to harness the fearsome power of the Nine-Tailed Fox chakra within him — as he prepares for the finals of the third phase of the Chûnin Selection Exams. Meanwhile, secret alliances are exposed, as it becomes clear that other ninja villages are plotting against Konohagakure...and Gaara's mysterious past is revealed!

AVAILABLE NOW!

Tegami Bachi
LETTER · BEE

a BEACON of hope for a world trapped in DARKNESS

1
VOLUME
SHONEN JUMP MANGA
Tegami Bachi
LETTER BEE
STORY AND ART BY
HIROYUKI ASADA
Tegami Bachi
HIROYUKI ASADA
viz

STORY AND ART BY
HIROYUKI ASADA

— Manga on sale now! —

You're Reading in the Wrong Direction!!

Whoops! Guess what? You're starting at the wrong end of the comic!

...It's true! In keeping with the original Japanese format, **Naruto** is meant to be read from right to left, starting in the upper-right corner.

Unlike English, which is read from left to right, Japanese is read from right to left, meaning that action, sound effects and word-balloon order are completely reversed...something which can make readers unfamiliar with Japanese feel pretty backwards themselves. For this reason, manga or Japanese comics published in the U.S. in English have sometimes been published "flopped"–that is, printed in exact reverse order, as though seen from the other side of a mirror.

By flopping pages, U.S. publishers can avoid confusing readers, but the compromise is not without its downside. For one thing, a character in a flopped manga series who once wore in the original Japanese version a T-shirt emblazoned with "M A Y" (as in "the merry month of") now wears one which reads "Y A M"! Additionally, many manga creators in Japan are themselves unhappy with the process, as some feel the mirror-imaging of their art alters their original intentions.

We are proud to bring you Masashi Kishimoto's **Naruto** in the original unflopped format. For now, though, turn to the other side of the book and let the ninjutsu begin...!

–Editor

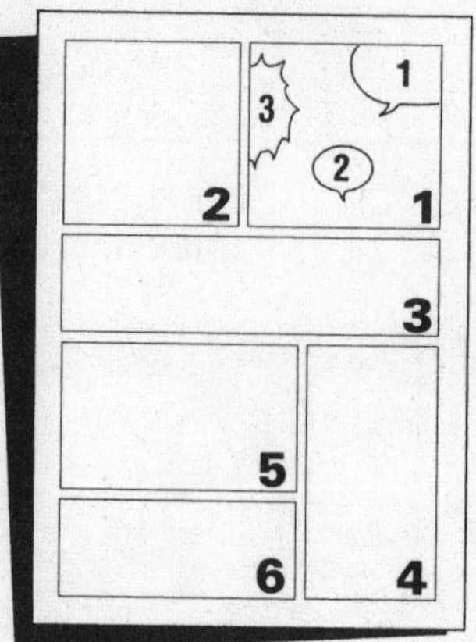
1
3
2
2
1
3
5
6
4